The Communities
and Can Regain

MICHAEL YOUNG is an eminent sociologist who is co-author (with Peter Willmott) of *Family and Kinship in East London*. He drafted Labour's 1945 Election Manifesto, "Let us Face the Future". Now in the House of Lords, he was the originator of the Consumers' Association and the Open University, as well as over 30 other social and voluntary enterprises. He is the Director of the Institute of Community Studies and an Hon. Fellow of the British Association.

GERARD LEMOS was for many years a senior manager in housing associations. Since 1990 he has been advising housing organisations, including many local authorities and housing associations, the Housing Corporation and the National Housing Federation. He has written and researched many articles, reports and books on social housing and is a respected analyst of and commentator on housing policy.

The Communities We Have Lost and Can Regain

Michael Young and Gerard Lemos

with research by Lesley Cullen

First published in Great Britain 1997
by Lemos & Crane
20 Pond Square
Highgate Village
London N6 6BA

© Lemos & Crane 1997

ISBN 1-898001-35-9

A CIP catalogue record for this book is available
from the British Library

Cover and book design by DAP Ltd, London

Printed and bound by Redwood Books, Trowbridge.

Acknowledgements

We would like to acknowledge with warmth the financial help received from the Housing Corporation. This project was carried out through funding from the Housing Corporation's Innovation and Good Practice Programme. The Anchor Trust also made a substantial financial contribution for which we are very grateful, particularly to John Belcher, through whose good offices the contribution was made. We have also incurred a large debt to many individuals. We have given a special place to Lesley Cullen who took charge of the survey itself. We have also been much helped by James Smith of the Institute of Community Studies, again with the survey and in many other ways. Further interviews were done by Tessa Dugmore of the Institute, Charlie Forman and Elaine Bowes of Lemos & Crane. The visits referred to in this book were either made by the authors or one of the researchers. Carwyn Gravell has done much patient and thorough editing at Lemos & Crane. In addition, we would like to thank the housing associations which took part in the survey, while stressing that the interpretation and use of the information they gave us is our responsibility. Our preliminary attempts at developing the ideas we write about here started with the new mutual aid housing scheme proposed in Bradford. The support and encouragement of Anil Singh at Manningham Housing Association and Linda Taylor at the Anchor Trust gave life to our initial thoughts. Finally we want to thank the many people in and out of the Housing Corporation who have been willing to discuss the issues with us. The views expressed do not necessarily represent the views of the Corporation. They are the responsiblity of the authors.

Contents

Foreword

In this book we address what is, to our minds, the most fundamental question facing social housing: what is a community and how can it be brought about?

We did not think for a moment when we began that we were the only people with these concerns on our mind. We now know that people have been thinking about and seeking to address this question all over the country. The search is on for new solutions to old problems. We have discovered some of these thoughts and ideas in our research.

We have made some proposals here about how social housing should be built, let and managed. We offer them for consideration by others, not in the expectation that they will be readily agreed to, but certain in the knowledge of a common wish for new approaches. We hope to further the debate to help us and others to develop a new purpose and new methods. This can only happen with the widest possible discussion and involvement. With this in mind, responses, comments, criticisms and suggestions will be very welcome.

CHAPTER One

Towards an Ethical Housing Policy

Secure housing for rent for people who cannot afford to buy their own home, or cannot find or afford a home to rent privately, is one of the great post-war social innovations. Many good houses have been built by local authorities and housing associations and contented people live in them, but few would suggest that the nation's housing is fit and ready for a new millenium. And it is not just social housing for rent about which we and others are concerned. A little of what has passed needs to be described to set the context for where we are now.

In the home ownership sector, once trumpeted as the engine of national prosperity through the generations, repeated cycles of boom and bust have resulted in people being unable to move when they want to because of negative equity and being forced to move when they do not want to as a result of mortgage repossessions. Because of repossessions in the early 1990s the largest forced eviction of people from their homes took place since the Highland Clearances in the 1830s.[1] Subsidies have been offered for home ownership in the form of mortgage interest tax relief and discounts on the right to buy council houses. Some people have bought homes which they could not afford.

At least 100,000 new homes for rent are projected to be needed every year in social housing for at least the next twenty years.[2] We have not approached that figure for many years. In the year to April 1997 Housing Corporation investment delivered 32,000 new homes for rent.[3] Too many people remain homeless and in need of housing: more than 134,000 households were accepted by local authorities as homeless in 1995.[4] Between December 1996 and March 1997, 1,693 people used shelters for rough sleepers in London – a 59 per cent increase on the previous winter.[5] Some housing is in disrepair and needs substantial investment, perhaps as much as £20 billion of it. The efforts that there have been to restore social housing and regenerate the inner city have only been a partial success. A plethora of unstrategic "schemes" that swallow large sums of public money, each a monument to transitory interests, has not succeeded in rebuilding communities, even when they have rebuilt housing. In 1989 the Audit Commission complained of a "patchwork quilt of complexity and idiosyncracy". Not too soon the Single Regeneration Budget has brought together no less than 20 other sources of government funds, many of which involved housing regeneration, each in a slightly different configuration: Housing Action Trusts, Estate Action, City Challenge, Urban Programme, Safer Cities, Task Force and on and on.[6] Despite combining these programmes the Audit Commission were still concerned in 1997, "The growth in the number of competitions for which authorities can bid has created the danger of a new patchwork effect. One director of housing itemised ten competitions that his department was bidding for or managing." Richard Caborn, the Minister of State at the Department for the Environment, Transport and the Regions, observed, "the competition for resources without a coherent regional strategy has become something of a beauty contest".[7] The new names and the 1980s' language of business cannot conceal falling funds.

Poor people find it harder than ever to make ends meet in social housing as rents rise, in part to repay the private borrowing that has been introduced into the funding of social housing since 1988. Unemployment passes from generation to generation in areas where major local employers have disappeared. Crime and anti-social behaviour have in some places become endemic;[8] not just in older social housing either. New housing built less than ten years ago has, in some instances, begun to take on the quality of the old "sink estates", at least partly because the shortage of new housing has meant that only the poorest and most needy have been able to get access to social housing at all. Stable communities have been hard to establish quickly in these circumstances.[9] The demographic mix of those in the greatest need has led to "bulges" of young people on estates, even new ones, with little to do but cause trouble.[10] The Housing Act 1988 brought private borrowing into housing associations and exposed them to previously unknown risks. Predicting and controlling building costs became a top priority. Some housing associations were tempted into buying estates at a fixed price which had already been built speculatively for private sale. Sometimes they have regretted it. Filled to the gunwales by families with children (living with paper-thin walls, an under-supply of play space and vast spaces to park the cars that the tenants do not own) some of the estates we visited, with accomodation designed for a couple, no children and a spare room for the computer, are scarcely fit for social housing.

Our proposals cannot counter all of these ills, some of them intractable and long-standing, though we will discuss them in more depth in Chapter 3 when we describe the building blocks of community, but we are sure, by developing a housing policy for people not buildings, recoveries are possible from many of these disasters. With so many hopes frustrated, with so many failures to log, policy-makers are liable to wash their hands of the whole subject and withdraw state policy from a battlefield on which it has been so scarred, not just here, but across Europe. Here is the view of one of our foremost observers of social housing, Anne Power, who for more than twenty years has charted most acutely the depredations of estates of mass housing.

> Europe is at a crossroads on many social and economic issues. Housing is central to the changes under way. The political dynamics surrounding housing, and particularly social housing, are conflictual. In Britain, homelessness and polarisation are highly charged issues, with deep social consequences. Elsewhere a more open debate ranges around social exclusion, poverty, unemployment, family break-up and the consequences of large-scale immigration, all linked to growing social problems on unpopular estates. The role of government in this context is controversial and sometimes provocative.[11]

Controversy and provocation there will be, but withdrawal of public policy there must not be. It would be like creating a disaster, then crying havoc and deserting the victims of the havoc, leaving them to look after themselves without any aid from the perpetrator. At its best, a new housing policy should embody a new and integrated approach to repairing some of the devastation.

A NEW PURPOSE FOR HOUSING POLICY

The claim of housing on the nation's attention is liable to be undermined by a lack of clarity on precisely the social purpose which housing policy should serve. The goals of the other three great high-spending social services are relatively obvious, and relatively clear, which is one reason they are high spending. The goal of education is to prepare children and young people for a future that is fulfilling both to themselves and to their society. The goal of the NHS is to maintain and improve health. The main goal of social security is to put a safety net under everyone's standard of life. This leaves the fourth great social service – housing – without an overarching goal which is so self-evidently compelling and consensual. Though there are many books, papers and publications which set out policies and goals, there is far from universal agreement.

In this book we are arguing that the re-creation and creation of community, with mutual aid being the kernel of community, is the overarching purpose to which housing policy should be marching as much in local authorities as in housing associations; in addition we propose some of the particular measures which could make it all happen. And we would want to see, as we explain, measures to encourage mutual aid to extend beyond social housing to all forms of housing and all kinds of community.

Housing policy is most apt for this high purpose. A house is a statement, as if in a kind of social body language, of the great issue before any society: what should be the balance between the individual and the collective? A house is also a home to which of all places on the surface of this globe the fortunate members of society most assuredly belong, something about which we may from time to time feel some ambivalence but none of which normally diminishes the sense of this being our place on the earth. Unless you are a Duke in a stately home, the home is person sized. It is highly individual on the inside, every possession signifying meaning and personal memory. It confers the only primary privacy which a citizen in a modern global world can contrive.

But the privacy also rests on a massive support system with multiple channels from that global world into the home. Without anyone to carry it, water is piped invisibly into your bathtaps from far distant reservoirs and if they are not refilled with their anticipated quota of rain, hoses for houses have to be forbidden for quite long periods, much to the annonyance particularly of people living in Yorkshire. Turn a tap and gas arrives unseen from the North Sea, flick a switch and electricity pulses in from power stations, pick up a receiver or turn on the TV set and what mind-boggling communications are waiting to flood into your eyes and ears! The reservoirs for these communications never suffer droughts.

The privacy is also dependent upon a hundred other privacies not intruding on one's own. For one house stands next to another, one flat immediately above another in which other people may be noisily expressing their individuality to everyone's exasperation but their own. The juxtaposition can produce an angry banging on the wall and the breaking off of diplomatic or any other relations. Or it can produce a scenario of neighbourliness.

> It is only one of the most remarkable of all social facts that, coming down from untold ages, there should be this instinctive understanding that the man who establishes his house besides yours begins to have a claim upon your sense of comradeship.[12]

That may be a bit over-optimistic when applied to our modern world. It is by no means universally true. There is a variant of Gresham's Law in mass communication – not that bad money drives out good but that bad news drives out good and it is bad news we have been getting about the state of neighbourliness. The issue about the kind of relationship you have with your neighbours is inescapable, and inescapably moral. A Robinson Crusoe does not need ethics because he does not need others. There cannot be a community of one. A resident of Thornton Heath or Wythenshawe cannot avoid ethics if she or he is to live amicably with the world around.

THE MEANS TOWARDS THE END

A housing policy underpinned by an ethical goal – the goal of community-building in which the good side of people's natures has a chance of fuller expression – can also help to fill a gap in current social policy. Politicians and pundits have not been sparing in their espousal of the need for community. In Chapter 3 we discuss the building blocks of community so yearned for. The same people have been rather less specific about the means that could be used to attain it. Housing policy is such a means.

British socialism not only owed more to Methodism than Marxism, it owed much more to the practice of mutual aid between working-class families than to doctrines of public ownership. This tradition of mutual aid goes back a long way to the friendly societies, sick clubs, slate clubs, co-operative societies and trade unions of the nineteenth century and beyond – a tradition which is being comprehensively overthrown by building societies and mutual insurance offices turning themselves into ordinary profit-seeking companies. But it is a tradition which can now be reinstated. Mutual aid was richly woven into the everyday exchanges between ordinary people. Here is George Lansbury speaking, the leader of the Labour Party in the mid-1930s.

> In working-class districts it is the neighbour next door or upstairs who helps the mother whose baby has arrived, when through unemployment or any other cause maternity benefit is not available. It is the same people who do the washing and clearing up when the mother of a family of little ones is laid aside. I like to remember my own mother, who for years never failed to give a Sunday dinner to old people who lived across the road. My brother and I very proudly trotted off with those little presents. At the same time, in another part of Whitechapel, my wife's mother was doing the same thing, and so indeed were thousands of equally thoughtful people throughout our land. Whatever the milk of human kindness there has been in me has come down from those early days when even a small boy could understand without any oral or other teaching what "love one another" meant.[13]

Lansbury's way of talking about mutual aid may sound old fashioned. It is a different society now. Could mutual aid really have any place in a society where more and more people seem to be out for themselves and for themselves alone? We believe it still exists and could be adapted to be as relevant to modern conditions as it ever was in the past.

SAVINGS FOR THE WELFARE STATE

E thics are often costly. But that drawback is not one from which a community policy should suffer. Rather the other way around – where there is a community which goes from being an area marked on a map to being a place that lives in the heart, people help each other. Mutual aid is at the heart of community, and while much of it costs nothing in money terms, there is a considerable cost if mutual aid is absent. If it is absent, people have to be paid to do what others might do for free, if it is to be done at all.

Paid people – doctors, nurses, social workers, paid carers – are unfailingly needed, and the need is not going to be reduced yet, or reduced by much. Every year modern medicine and a modern standard of life are keeping alive millions of people who would in the past have died from this or that disease which has now been vanquished or, more often, not vanquished but expensively held in check; and every year more and more people, particularly women, live on beyond their three score years and ten. All of this requires professional people to continue the benign work of saving and extending life and improving the quality of life. So there may be no vast savings on present levels of expenditure to be extracted from the efforts to rebuild communities; but at least it should be possible to hold down the cost of care. The Institute of Actuaries expects the number of disabled people will rise from 6.4 million in 1991 to 8.5 million in 2031. Demography is the enemy of the Treasury. Old people live longer but sometimes with a disability or needing care. But community can be the Treasury's friend. Expenditure on housing has the very special property to it that when spent in such a way as to expand mutual aid, there should be a yield on the investment in terms of money saved on the costs of care, as well as a yield in human kindness. And if, as it seems, there are going to be more people who need care or support, making money spent now go as far as possible in the future is much to be welcomed.

In this respect housing as a social service is on a par with education. Housing and education are social services on which the net return can be larger than the net expenditure. They are in the "spend to save" category – in this respect they are like the £800 million which the former Chancellor of the Exchequer, Kenneth Clarke, wanted to spend over three years on measures to tackle fraud in order to save more than £6 billion eventually.[14] The Labour Government too believes it is possible to spend to save in some circumstances. They are spending on anti-fraud measures to reduce, for example, prescription fraud and indeed fraud and mismanagement of Housing Benefit. In 1996 according to an estimate by the Department for Social Security, £900 million of Housing Benefit may be being overpaid, out of a total budget of £12 billion. A joint study by the Audit Commission and the National Audit Office revealed "that councils have responded vigorously to subsidy incentives which encourage them to investigate and detect fraud".[15] A little has been spent and a good deal may yet be saved. Expenditure on social security, vital as that also is to any society which is justifiably called a caring society, does not necessarily recoup itself, and new incentives are needed to take people from welfare to work.

But expenditure on education can produce a return over people's lifetimes which is far greater than the input; and housing can be the same. Housing expenditure can save money by preventing and reducing ill-health and enabling communities to flourish, their members looking after one another, neighbours, friends and family.

The facts about present dispositions were set out in a 1996 survey.[16] The value of informal community care is calculated according to how much it would cost to replace the informal with paid people at the average cost of household help. The figures come from the General Household Survey. The summary is in Table 1 below.

■ *Table 1.* **Care Costs (£ billion)**

	1995	2011	2031
Formal Costs (paid from public & private sources)	12	17.6	33.1
Cost to Taxpayer	8.8	9.7	13.1
Notional Monetary Cost of Informal Care	33.8	34.6	31.7

Note: This does not include what is spent by parents in the normal run of bringing up children.

Notice the figures attributed to informal care. Currently, it is, at over £33 billion, four times greater than the cost to the taxpayer. This refers for the most part to the care provided by members of families who are paid not in money but in terms of affection and a sense of duty done. In 1990 16 per cent of the population were carers and some 1.5 million adults in Great Britain were spending more than 20 hours a week on caring.[17] Much of it is given by people in the Third Age, men as well as women over 55 or those who have retired from ordinary work and still have many years of active life ahead of them before they are in need of care themselves. A MORI survey for Anchor Trust in 1996 found 17 per cent of people over retirement age caring or supporting someone else. Nine per cent were caring for a sick or disabled partner, six per cent for a relative older than themselves and two per cent supporting other relatives.[18] If informal family care were to disappear, or even to diminish as much in the next 40 years as it has in the last 40, the population time bomb could blow a gaping hole in the finances of the state.

It is not just in the care of the old and the disabled that people have sometimes to be paid to do what many others do for free. Men have for many centuries been able to go to work because women looked after their children. Now women too have increasingly gone to work, and this has partly been made possible by the support given in the care of children by grandparents as well as paid providers, paid mostly by the parents.

FORMS OF MUTUAL AID

We are using the term mutual aid rather widely in this book, so to end this first chapter we should say something about the various meanings of the term as it circles through the book and outwards from two people to three people and then out to broader and broader groups which eventually embrace the whole of society.

The first and most humble meaning is of more or less simultaneous reciprocity between two people. A gives B a kiss and B gives it back. A looks after B when B is ill and B looks after A when A is ill.

The second and less humble meaning is *lagged reciprocity* when there are time-lags in the process. The most fundamental time-lag which keeps the whole together is when a parent looks after a child. It is at the time mostly one-way aid. But even though affection descends more readily than it ascends, parents giving it most readily to children, there can be some return traffic of care and feeling later on when the child looks after the parent. This is mutual aid given and received at different points in the course of the life cycle. Mutual aid in the prime of life is a repayment of the debts incurred in childhood and a down payment on the care that might be needed in old age. Friends and neighbours might help one another too with no immediate return, but with a strong implicit presumption of help to be returned at an unspecified moment of future need.

The third and still less humble meaning is where mutuality

becomes multilateral – three ways, or four ways or n-ways. A helps B. B helps C. C helps A. This multilateral mutual aid can be stretched, say, from a few people in a savings club to include millions of people who are unknown but, though unknown, contribute to the welfare of each and everyone of us. At its furthest extent this is the mutuality of humankind, without which there would be no humankind. We are all our brother's keeper and our brother or our sister is the keeper of us all.

The first two kinds of meaning lend themselves to a calculus of self-interest. Do something for another now and get something back now. Do something for another now and get something back in the future – though members of families do not often even make the calculation. A parent does not care for an ailing child in the expectation of getting a finely calculated repayment in sixty years' time.

For multilateral exchanges of aid and support there is not even the chance of calculating self-interest. People are sometimes so moved, or angered by the indignities, the cruelties or the hardship they see around them that they give generously, financially and of their time and energy. When they do so, it does not generally pass through their minds that they have taken out a tiny insurance policy against the unhappiness that they may in the future experience as the result of crime, vandalism or violence. The connection is so slight that self-interest is not even worth thinking about. Multilateral but inescapable and necessary mutual aid has in these circumstances become altruism, and that is still much in evidence. The giving of blood by volunteers continues to be the best example of widespread altruism on the part of the many to help the few; help given to a few strangers to boot. This "gift relationship" is more safe, more plentiful and engages more people than ever it would if donors were paid for their blood. The relationship is voluntary and multilateral mutual aid which may, if the need for blood should arise in a donor, also be lagged reciprocity, a possibility scarcely contemplated at the point of giving.[19]

So much by way of introduction. We describe the flagship mutual aid housing proposal in Bradford in Chapter 5 below. It could be a demonstration of what the principles of mutual aid might mean in practice. In this book we are drawing a distinction between formal mutual aid – activities encouraged and enabled by interventions of social policy and public and voluntary services – and informal mutual aid which takes place without the encouragement or intervention of formal agencies between families, neighbours, friends, people with shared interests, a common religion or culture or those facing a common adversity. In Chapter 2 on formal mutual aid we will report on our survey of what some housing associations already do beyond the primary task of building and good management of social housing. In Chapter 3 we will offer an account of the conditions which favour the development of a community in which people are good citizens to each other; in which informal mutual aid thrives. To our minds the existence of informal mutual aid – the bonds and ties by which people are united in a community – can be built upon by formal social policy and public and voluntary activities. Or informal mutual aid can be undermined by the same agencies acting sometimes with good intentions, but producing unintended destructive consequences for those existing bonds and ties. Chapter 3 also describes some of what has happened in housing policy with, we believe, deleterious results for mutual aid. In Chapter 4 we will propose some formal interventions for the encouragement of informal mutual aid. In Chapter 5 we will apply some of the principles of mutual aid to the wider community beyond social housing.

Formal Mutual Aid in Housing Associations

We are going to start with the survey we made of existing housing associations. We wanted to find out what they are doing to start up new bodies, projects or activities to meet the needs of their tenants and, in some cases, people who are not their tenants. Insofar as they have gone beyond building and managing houses, they are fostering mutual aid of the multilateral kind as we have defined it.

The history of local authority estates and efforts to regenerate them in the context of increased social polarisation has been written up in a stream of excellent reports by Anne Power. In a 1995 report, written with Rebecca Tunstall, Power described the conditions she saw on 20 of the worst council estates in 1979 and 1980:

> dirty, chaotic, impoverished, vandalised, hard to let, unrepaired islands of neglect. Boarded-up properties, a massive exodus of tenants, very few if any trained staff, low demand, and no contact point between tenants and landlords, made the estates unpopular, vulnerable and sometimes out of control.[1]

And there were in Power's estimation some 2,000 of these estates in the UK. Intensive management reforms were put in place. Staff worked from local offices, given the freedom to innovate and cut through red tape to manage lettings, repairs and caretaking. Tenants had an open door at the office and police officers returned to the beat. All most welcome and at the time, effective. But these efforts were almost overwhelmed by the social and economic changes of the 1980s. The worst was yet to come.

> Declining estates experienced tumultuous change along-side management reforms. They were close to the bottom of the social pecking order. The lack of formal jobs and rapid growth in lone parenthood increased dependence amongst council tenants. Concentrations of black people on unpopular estates grew, particularly in London. Exploding home ownership drew many stable households out of renting, turning estates into "welfare islands" – most people on these estates could not buy even if they wanted to. The financial and social gap between council housing and the majority of the country increased rapidly, and the worst estates were worse than most council housing.[2]

In 1997 Power has raised an even darker spectre – the possibility of widespread civil disorder. In the summers of 1991 and 1992 there were 13 serious disorders in residential areas, characterised as riots by the press. Unlike most of the riots of the 1980s, 12 of the 13 occurred on council estates. She and Rebecca Tunstall have concluded, "more episodes of disorder in social housing estates are inevitable unless we tackle residualisation and shift service provision to proactive prevention".[3]

The introduction of private finance into housing associations in 1988 brought the need to manage risk, as we said in the last chapter. As a consequence, rehabilitating street properties became less the norm, superseded in many places by the building of new estates. More houses and flats could be built quickly at a fixed price. As local authorities stopped building they became less able to meet their obligations to find homes for homeless people and others in housing need. Housing associations, with their new estates, were called upon to fill the breach, receiving nominations from the council to their new estates. They had to house a greater proportion of those in the greatest need than had previously ever been required of them.

Two reports by David Page published in 1993 and 1994[4] brought housing associations up short against a new possibility. As a consequence of all that had happened through the 1980s housing associations were storing up for themselves the same problems with the new housing estates they were building that local authorities had earlier visited on themselves, perhaps unwittingly, and their tenants. Page set out concerns which were new to housing associations. Nonetheless the sentiments he expressed resonated widely. According to Page, these problems are not the result of the demerits of local authorities as landlords when compared with housing associations. Instead, the difficulties stem from the design of some social housing – not just unpopular high rise, but low space standards and poor facilities for children to play; where that housing is located – living on peripheral estates making it much more difficult for tenants to take a full part in the life of town or city, particularly its employment opportunities; tenant selection and allocations and estate management. In his second report Page suggested a range of possible preventative and corrective actions: planning for a social balance; the need for an informal social infrastructure alongside the formal infrastructure of schools, shops and transport; intervention in the first two years after tenants have moved in; community development and initiatives which "add value", which "enable low-income households to choose some of the benefits normally available to those with greater economic power".[5] We welcome all of that, but in our view a further mile is needed to build and re-build communities. Stability of residence, the presence of three or four generations and mutual aid, both formal and informal, are also called for. These other building blocks of strong communities are discussed more fully in Chapter 3.

With some of these concerns in mind, the Housing Corporation launched the Housing Plus initiative in 1994. Since then housing associations have been encouraged to look beyond the more straightforward issues of housing management, over and above lettings, rent collection, repairs, maintenance and settling neighbour disputes. The wider needs and aspirations of their tenants should, suggested the Housing Corporation, also feature in the plans of housing associations. This is how the Housing Corporation has defined what they mean by Housing Plus.

A Housing Plus approach comprises the following elements:

- Its objective is the creation and maintenance of sustainable social housing.
- Its focus is on ensuring that social housing works with and contributes positively to the community in which it is located.
- Its agents are both the management and development functions of housing associations and other registered social landlords in partnership with residents, local authorities and other service providers.
- Its benefit is the added value which accrues from the use of social housing resources which contribute to sustainability.

For social housing, sustainability can be defined as *"social housing which enjoys a continuous healthy demand for letting throughout its projected lifetime, without substantial unplanned expenditure"*.[6]

They have suggested a range of possible activities for housing associations (some of them outside the funding parameters of the Housing Corporation), including neighbourhood watch, allocation of housing to achieve an age balance, residential and nursing homes, adult literacy training, transport provision, and facilitating credit unions. Housing associations have the freedom to be creative. Backed up by innovation and good practice grants from the Housing Corporation they can respond over a larger canvas to the lives and needs of their tenants. Some of them have been able to do their bit about more general social problems, such as unemployment, which certainly affect their tenants and a great many other people besides.

The larger housing associations particularly have gone further and taken on a social investment role. In the case of Focus Housing Association in the Midlands, social investment, not just providing and managing good quality and affordable homes, has been proposed as their new core purpose. Richard Clark, the Chief Executive of Focus, puts it like this, "You can't say, 'Oh, and by the way we are going to alleviate poverty as well as building houses.' It has to start from fundamental principles and be planned as one strategy."[7] Irwell Valley Housing Association has proposed a radical extension to the services they offer tenants. Tenants who pay their rent on time, look after their home and have no history of anti-social behaviour will be offered a "Heart of Gold" service. This will include scholarships, apprenticeships, day trips, bank-rate interest on their rent accounts and discounts on food and household goods. Tenants who do not comply will be denied access to these services. The intention is to "dramatically re-invent" housing management and to "rock our industry's foundations", to promote a "self-help" ethos amongst tenants and say to anti-social tenants, "you've got to change your behaviour". The Chief Executive, Tom Manion, commented, "These goods and services will be delivered by our staff, who will be liberated from the negative activities of rent collection, eviction, empty property filling etc." The plans were based on "philanthropy, utilitarianism and reciprocity."[8] Radical thinking is clearly in the air.

We carried out a survey and more detailed follow-up case studies to enquire into their activities which contributed to mutual aid and building sustainable communities as these were seen by the staff of housing associations themselves. Our survey was of the largest 200 housing associations, as well as a random sample of 50 smaller ones.[9] We had a response rate of 56 per cent overall.[10] The larger the associations, the higher the rate of response, varying from 70 per cent of the largest 50 to 42 per cent of the sample of smaller associations, the latter generally having fewer community building projects to report.

As well as following up on some of the projects referred to in the responses to the survey, we also wrote up case studies of a few other projects which were not initiated by housing associations but contributed to building communities. Job creation and the use of local labour, the care and support of people with special needs and a credit union were looked into.

MUTUAL AID AND COMMUNITY-BUILDING

Because we see mutual aid, informal as well as formal, as intrinsic to community spirit, we asked housing associations whether they thought they should be encouraging it. Two thirds of those who filled in the questionnaire did not respond to this question at all. A small number were very definitely negative, at least in what they said. One housing association chief executive comments, "there is a considerable danger that associations over-reach themselves in talk about rebuilding communities". He accuses housing associations of having "a predilection…to make 'regeneration' efforts just another development project, rather than seeing themselves a little more humbly as bit players in a much larger drama, and tackling rather more humdrum issues in their own backyard".

That was one of the most admirably humble but not so admirably negative remarks.

On the other hand a housing association community development worker we interviewed on a visit commented, "No-one else is going to do it. I am very clear about this. The world has changed – at one time there were community workers; there were grant-based community associations; there were social workers and people out there doing this, but they are not there anymore. There is no-one else."

Most of the one third that ventured opinions were fairly positive, but there were plenty of caveats. One thought it was a "noble" idea, but gave a page of reasons why it was not practically possible, mostly to do with the lack of available funding; eleven used the word "should" but in the future tense; one said their association was being "pushed" in this direction. Twenty-two per cent of those that responded to the question wondered where the resources would come from, financial and otherwise. Here is a fairly typical view.

> Housing association developments are built solely with housing in mind and it is assumed that the surrounding community will somehow absorb them...I would agree that housing associations should encourage mutual aid and sustainable communities but would ask "who will fund and support it?" and "what role are the Housing Corporation prepared to play in it?"

But was it the social landlord's job at all? One respondent said, "Sometimes local authorities criticise housing associations for not making any social provision. They don't realise HAs are not funded for this in the same way as councils. Instead, the issue should be to acknowledge that our tenants are rate payers and concentrate on ways of integrating them into LA provision." Another association commented, "There is a temptation on statutory organisations to withdraw from their responsibilities when they see other agencies providing a lead and we must encourage and motivate others rather than replace them." There is a feeling amongst respondents that councils, with their strategic and enabling responsibilities for housing, education, social services and community services, should take the lead in community-building. Lack of resources in recent years has held back many local authorities from doing more, as they surely would have liked to.

More positively, some associations took a pragmatic view of the potential benefits: "essential for long-term viability"; "stock preservation, ease (and therefore reduced cost) of management, attractive to potential stock transfer tenants and landlords"; "safeguarding our rent stream". A very small number go further than that. One association describes promoting sustainable communities as "a core function". Another says it is "vital", and one of their three corporate objectives.

Older housing trusts, such as Peabody, took their responsibility for community-building extremely seriously. Housing associations formed out of the large scale voluntary transfers (LSVT) of housing associations stock also communicated strong and determined views. One commented, "LSVT Housing Associations have a particular responsibility as they own and manage the historic social housing in their transferring local authority district." These two types of organisations – LSVTs and older trusts – are the ones with the greatest number of estates to manage.

To summarise the general reactions: those who are for sustainable communities are by and large pragmatically keen, recognising the benefits to themselves and to their tenants. Those who are not sure, worry about the cost and the relevance to their "main work". Some see mutual aid and sustainable communities as none of their business. There is still much to be done to convince housing associations that they could and, more crucially, should play an active community development role, along with local authorities.

WORKING IN PARTNERSHIP

One kind of collaboration has taken place in the North Kensington City Challenge in West London which we visited. The neighbourhood contains social housing, home owners and a small amount of privately rented housing. Three social landlords bid for funds – two housing associations and the local authority, and they, along with local people and other community organisations, were all involved in running the many activities and gatherings at the newly established Residents Information Centre. The Centre was a focus for local people to have their say in the comprehensive redevelopment, not just of their housing, but the entire neighbourhood. Improvements have been made to many homes over the years of the City Challenge; residents feel a greater sense of safety from crime; there is a less alarming traffic flow, a reduction in neglected verminous rubbish and better play facilities for children, as well as more local employment opportunities in businesses set up by local people. On top of all of that, a greater sense of community is felt by many local people towards their fellow residents. Much that has been done would not even remotely have fallen within traditional notions of housing management.

Not that everything has gone smoothly. The community development staff were funded by housing associations but they were reluctant to permit them to report directly to the community forum. A compromise was found. Tenants have been involved in all staff appointments, often advising on job descriptions, insisting all jobs are advertised in the local press and they are always represented at interview. But the housing association has in turn insisted that appointment and line management should remain their responsibility. This wish not to break the link between funding, employment and accountability is a rather general one. Perhaps people feel that blurring lines of accountability will surely end in conflict rather than partnership. Admittedly, tenants' groups and local community groups are sometimes joined less to their landlord by mutual aid than by mutual suspicion. But in the case of North Kensington, because of the considerable diplomatic skills of the staff, along with their very remarkable capacity for lateral thinking out of new solutions, it was not like that. The staff, in the way they have dealt with colleagues and local residents, explaining themselves carefully to everyone, seeking to avoid and resolve conflicts between individuals and organisations, finding compromises where available, but being assertive when required, have satisfied many types of accountability, both formal and informal.

Despite all the difficulties, the best way of proceeding is for agencies to work together. The worst breakdowns we encountered were where there was only a housing association involved and it had lost the backing of its tenants. On one estate we visited the tenants felt that an extensive consultation about estate re-design had been a sham because many of their suggestions had not been acted upon, even though a very extensive programme of building works was due to begin. The local estate manager could offer little explanation. Those decisions had been taken by another department of the association. No amount of money, only a good deal of openness, time and effort, can revive trust once it has been lost.

It cannot be wrong for housing associations to co-operate in activities which do not benefit their own tenants, or which benefit other people as well. Their tenants should not be isolated from the wider community and it is surely part of the housing association's role to ensure that they are not.

COMMUNITY-BUILDING PROJECTS

So what projects are undertaken by housing associations beyond their main function of building and managing homes? They were asked whether there were projects or activities, either of their own or in co-operation with others, which in their view contributed to mutual aid and a sustainable community. One hundred and nineteen housing associations (86 per cent of respondents) answered the question, and told us all together about 684 projects/activities on their sites. They described 278 of them in detail.

The most general point to make about the ones described is that they were on the whole of rather recent origin, as shown in Table 2 below. The Housing Corporation's Housing Plus initiative in 1994, described above, has evidently had an influence.

■ *Table 2.* **Length of operation of projects**

Years of operation	Projects	Percentage of projects
Under 1	84	31
1 – 2	64	24
2 – 5	66	24
More than 5	58	21

Note: We were not told how long ago 6 of the 278 projects described were started

Although there has clearly been a recent expansion – a third were started in the last year – some date much further back. Meeting the needs of elderly and disabled people were the most long-established activities. Forty-nine per cent of projects for elderly people and 33 per cent for people with disabilities were established more than five years ago. Just 17 per cent of community and neighbourhood associations, 23 per cent of community facilities and 17 per cent of child-care projects were established more than five years ago. The vast majority of youth and employment generation projects – foyers, skills training and local labour initiatives – date from two to five years ago.

The projects that housing associations identified as contributing to the building of sustainable communities fell broadly into five categories:[11] firstly, tenant involvement and community facilities; secondly, projects for elderly and disabled people; thirdly, projects designed to benefit children and young people; fourthly, employment generation; fifthly, credit unions and local exchange trading schemes

(LETS). The numbers in each category are shown in Table 3 below.

■ *Table 3.* **Projects and activities on housing association sites**

	Projects/ activities	Percentage of total projects
Tenant involvement and community facilities	216	34.7
Care for elderly and disabled people	179	28.7
Employment generation	139	22.3
Children and youth	77	12.4
Credit unions and LETS	12	1.9
Total	623	100
		(rounded down)

Working with tenants, neighbourhood and community associations and providing community facilities featured large. The largest contribution to community-building was made by these activities according to the sponsoring housing associations. Fifty-eight per cent of projects providing community facilities were established in the last two years; so while for some there is a long-standing commitment, for others it is quite new.

Tenant involvement

Mutual aid is in many circumstances best provided informally by people themselves with their friends and relatives as we discussed in Chapter 1. With that in mind one might expect to see extensive tenant involvement in the initiation of the projects to build sustainable communities. Not true, however. Much of this activity is top down: 69 per cent of the projects that housing associations told us about were initiated by staff alone, with only 21 per cent of projects having tenants involved in the initiation. Seventeen per cent of those who replied said that tenants associations were involved in management.

Support for community and neighbourhood associations was given by 68 per cent of housing associations. Seventeen per cent of the projects had been going for more than five years, so the support sometimes had a long history; however, nearly a quarter were established within the last year. But much of the encouragement for tenants was not, it would seem, aimed at involving tenants in their neighbourhoods and communities. The primary objective was often involving tenants in the governance of the housing association itself. The National Housing Federation code of governance[12] has clearly had an impact in further encouraging housing associations to put tenants on their boards of management. In one association training was given to help tenants "to better understand the environment in which we operate as a provider of housing and to consult them on how they would like us to do things better". Another had gone to the extent of establishing five tenants' associations, arranging meeting places for them, and allocating a budget of £50,000 for environmental improvements in neighbourhoods identified by tenants' associations. The association described the purpose of all this activity as "a means for nomination of tenants to the association's board of management and also to provide channels for dialogue on all our policies, activities and service delivery". In this prescription the purpose of tenant participation is more consumer feedback rather than community development.

This increased interest in consulting and involving tenants has led in some places to the development of estate agreements. These are renewable agreements made between landlords and tenants of a particular area setting out the standards of service provided to tenants and priorities for action. "Estate agreements could stimulate more formal tenant participation in estate management as well as including greater numbers of tenants in dealing directly with their landlords," according to Joseph Rowntree research.[13]

On the Shipfield estate in Norfolk, which we visited, there is a highly active tenants' association. It was established in the middle 1980s on an estate that was built thirty years ago. Five of the original residents are still there. Most residents have lived there for at least ten years. Sixty-five residents are members of the association, about two thirds of the households living on the estate. The association is run by an energetic committee of about ten people, mostly made up of recently retired and very active pensioners. The leaders of the tenants' association play a befriending role to new arrivals, such as single mothers. So here is one of the long-established elements of all strong communities: namely, the presence of three generations, which we discuss in more detail in Chapter 3. The interests and care of children are guarded by people of grandparent age, not just by their parents' generation. This is informal mutuality, but generated through the formal structure of the tenants' association. Aside from these informal support arrangements, there are also the more formal activities of "homewatch", an anti-crime neighbourhood watch scheme, and organised fun days and Christmas parties to which the home owners from the edge of the estate also come. In this case the establishment of the tenants' association, the provision of the community space and an enabling and supportive attitude on the part of the landlord was much praised by tenants.

It is clearly not always so easy. On another estate we visited which had been beset by crime, the residents' association had a great deal of difficulty in keeping going. A whole range of activities had met largely with apathy – mother and toddlers' group, health education classes and so on. A food purchasing co-op which bought and sold food more cheaply than the estate shop had struggled to get going. The one activity for which there was considerable support was the regular car boot sale. Even so some tenants were still committed and had an eye to mutual aid, though they did not use the term. One idea from the tenants' association was to recycle cast-off fridges and cookers to those without the means to buy them for themselves.

There are many reasons for success or failure of tenants' associations. A very active core group of tenants may get things moving, but they may also be seen as excluding and unwelcoming. The most persistent problem mentioned to us, particularly on our visits, was a lack of trust both amongst the residents themselves, and between the residents and the landlord. On one estate we visited, the lack of play-space for the ten year-olds was the big issue. The large housing association, despite many an entreaty from the tenants' association, would not contribute money, equipment or space; if the landlord disregards community needs tenants and housing managers will surely ultimately pay a high price in broken windows, tenant complaints and possibly worse. On another estate we visited, a highly successful tenant management organisation had brought a vandalised and degraded estate back into use by doing some of the building work themselves. So far, so good. They then built a community/employment training centre. But the funding was dependent on promoting successful employment initiatives which the tenants did not have all the skills to deliver. At the same time tenants wanted – but have not got – funding for the administration of the centre community's functions. The unresolved ensuing tensions are reflected in poor relationships between the tenants, the centre staff and the landlord.

Providing community facilities in the form of buildings is, notwithstanding the problems we have mentioned, still common. Sixty-six per cent of responding housing associations did so. This is particularly marked on large multi-landlord estates, such as Windsor Park in

Beckton, East London and Davidson Road in South London. Even on older estates, it is becoming more common to convert an empty flat or shop into a community meeting place. The use of these facilities has more to do with what tenants want, and bringing tenants together, than the approach taken to involving tenants in governance.[14]

The Meadowview Community Project in Brighton is on a new estate built by a consortium of housing associations. The largest number of homes was built by Sanctuary Housing, but the manager of Sanctuary's Brighton and Hove office commented to the local newspaper, "There is more than building houses and providing homes. It is a community development project, combining housing and community needs for the benefit of everybody living here." The community centre houses a youth club, a junior club and a parent and toddler group. A pre-school group meets there four times a week. A summer play scheme is scheduled, as are line dancing and aerobics classes. The community project has been funded in part by an innovation and good practice grant from the Housing Corporation. The community worker commented, "Basically every group is geared towards the residents learning to run those things themselves...We have around 60 volunteers, which from around 280 homes is a really positive commitment." The newly formed residents' association works with the housing associations and will work on the small, significant matters of quality of life, signposting and street cleaning for example. The steering group will eventually become a residents' management committee through which residents will become informal trustees of the project and the centre. The estate workers will, it is hoped, eventually be employed by the trustees. So, principles of community development and tenant participation in estate management and governance are being brought together. In our view, this is a more important set of objectives than electing a small number of tenants' representatives to the board of management, worthy though that may be for reasons of open governance, but it is not so important for the building of sustainable communities.

One housing association has given over a hard-to-let studio flat in a tower block to community use. Apart from being used by the residents' association, the flat is also used by the local job centre, Afro-caribbean luncheon club and mental health support group. Housing managers also hold surgeries there. All of these activities involve people from off the estate as well as on and, in the minds of the staff of the housing association, the activities have the effect of "knitting the estate into the local community". Bringing social housing tenants together with other local residents, regardless of the tenure of their homes, is clearly an important priority for building sustainable multi-tenure communities.

ELDERLY AND DISABLED PEOPLE

Seventy-eight per cent of housing associations made provision for older people and 71 per cent for disabled people. Half the projects we were told about for elderly people and one third of those for disabled people had been established more than five years ago. But only six per cent of projects for older people and those with disabilities involved tenants at the initial stage. The Housing Act 1974 was the landmark for the establishment of housing associations based in the community rehabilitating older properties often in multi-tenure neighbourhoods. These new associations, established at the time of growing concern about homelessness which we describe in the next chapter, certainly contributed to meeting the needs of the homeless. But until 1979 the role of many housing associations was to complement rather than substitute for local authorities. Housing for single people, old people and people with special needs were growth areas. These long-standing commitments are evidence of that original complementary role. Homeless and other families were for many years housed largely by local authorities. It was not until the 1980s that housing associations began to play a more inclusive role in providing for families of all kinds.

The Peabody Trust, one of the original Victorian philanthropic trusts with a large stock of estate-based housing, told us that it had made its own survey of elderly people living in "general needs" housing on its Shaftesbury Park Estate in Wandsworth, South London. Many had lived there all their adult lives, some since birth. Seventy-one per cent of the residents were interested in the idea of a "mobile warden". In response Peabody developed its Community Volunteers Project. People on the estate needing support and those able to provide it are known to the project. The volunteers are either young people, or "young old" people, members of the Third Age – between the ages of 60 and 75 – they are befriending those who are isolated or housebound, mostly those in their Fourth Age, over 75 and increasingly frail. They "bring friendship and support to the housebound and a feeling of being needed to the more mobile" and "formalise the good neighbour networks already in place". Having young volunteers helps "to bridge the generation gap". The project illustrates two building blocks of informal mutual aid which we will discuss in Chapter 3 – assisting people to remain in their own homes where they have been for a long time and finding people nearby from other generations to help them, even where the housing in which they live is not specifically designated for a specific group with a particular kind of need.

We also visited KeyRing. Operating in several London boroughs, the purpose of the project is to encourage independent living for people with learning difficulties in social housing, partly through mutual support between residents as part of the care package. Ten people with learning difficulties live in independent flats near but not adjacent to one another. They sign an agreement promising "to be a good neighbour to other KeyRing tenants and try to help if they have a problem." It seems to have worked, and there are other benefits too. One of the workers commented that, because the flats are not in one block but dispersed across the neighbourhood, the residents are well known in the local community; they are not institutionally segregated. She commented about one resident, "Too many people around here know him for anyone to get away with hurting him." Two residents have recently got married – an example of the move from community to kinship that we will discuss in Chapter 3. Many dispersed schemes for people with special needs were reported to us, suggesting a real wish on the part of social landlords to combine community integration with avoiding the dangers of isolation and institutionalisation.

EMPLOYMENT GENERATION

The next group of projects are the most recent ones, those designed to generate employment and relieve poverty: local labour schemes, employment skills training, establishing community businesses and "foyers". Most of these projects have been set up since the Housing Corporation's Housing Plus initiative in 1994.

Our respondents had set up either on their own or in partnership 26 foyers (of the 50 in the country as a whole), 49 local labour initiatives, and 45 skills training initiatives. Activities to generate employment for local people were almost exclusively jobs or traineeships in building and construction, a notoriously cyclical industry offering only unstable employment to many involved. Only one project was designed to train people for office jobs which the housing association itself might eventually offer to them. Four out of five people trained for office jobs on this project went on to secure them. The same project was also giving training in child care. Another offered training leading potentially to an NVQ in care. Training in gardening, ground maintenance and car mechanics was also given by one housing association.

Housing associations and local authorities are clearly major investors in the construction industry not just in new building but also rehabilitation and renovation. During the years of the recession in the late 1980s and early 1990s, housing associations were the only ones doing any building of new homes at all in many parts of the country. Expenditure on new building, repairs and maintenance is also for many associations the lion's share of their annual spending. Using that investment to employ local people on small maintenance or large building contracts, keeping the money spent by the association circulating in the local community, has obvious benefits. Public investment used to employ local people in areas of high unemployment may also redistribute wealth from richer to poorer areas, though taking a job from a person who does not live nearby and giving it to a local person clearly adds nothing to the national wealth. That can only be done by creating jobs in new and valuable products and services.

We visited Newham Wise in East London, a subsidiary of the Wise Group which was started in Glasgow in 1983. Area regeneration is combined with elements of a local labour initiative and job training. A year's training is given to local long-term unemployed people, many of whom are tenants of social housing, mainly in environmental improvement schemes in the community such as landscaping and construction. The training is primarily on the job, with day release to college, and results in an NVQ level 2 and, in some cases, NVQ level 3. Funding for Newham Wise comes mainly from the European Social Fund, contracts for environmental improvements from the London Borough of Newham, Energy Action Grants from central government and training contracts from London East TEC.

As they see it, Newham Wise has two sets of customers: the trainees and the organisations for which it is carrying out contracts. Forty-five per cent of those who start the training get a job on leaving. This figure rises to 70 per cent of those who complete the full year of the course. Newham Wise wants to increase employability. They measure this over three months, because a job for a week is not a real improvement in prospects. There is a substantial cost to providing training, so it is difficult to compete with other contractors on price but they can provide added value to their customers. An enormous amount of research in business schools has shown that customers take into account quality and innovation, not just price, and will sometimes pay a higher financial price for added value, so Newham Wise is swimming with the tide of contemporary management thinking.[15] Consultation with residents near where they are working is standard. Leaflets are delivered and they attend residents' associations meetings. "The friendly contractor" is the image they want. New landscaping is not just established and then left. They return to maintain it and work with the community, trying to prevent it being vandalised. Being local helps – a long-term commitment can be offered. The maintenance of some gardens are, over a period of time, handed over to local residents, but "changing attitudes is slow", they told us. Apart from working on estates, they work with community groups and schools – digging a pond for one school and making a garden for another.

This commitment to a partnership with the local community appears to work. A recent evaluation of the Wise Group by the Joseph Rowntree Foundation concluded that 36 per cent of residents were more satisfied with insulation work done by Newham Wise than work done in the past by the local council. None were less satisfied.

> The aim of creating greater attachment to a neighbourhood among the residents is perhaps an ambitious scheme and it is also a difficult outcome to quantify. The household survey has shown a great deal of positive impact on people's attitudes.[16]

Foyers[17] are a good example of housing associations working with other agencies. Foyers are about breaking the no-home/no-job cycle. Young people who were formerly homeless are offered housing and then set on the road to jobs with training. Foyers received funding from a variety of sources – the Housing Corporation, TECs, City Challenge, European Social Fund and others. But the motives for organisations to work together are not just financial. There is also value in blending insights and skills. We visited Camberwell Foyer in South London. Once young people without work are nominated to the foyer they are vetted to ensure that they are sufficiently motivated; if not, they are not given a place. In the foyer the young person puts together an action plan with a vocational counsellor. If they do not attend the training courses in the action plan, they are asked to leave the foyer. So there is both screening at the beginning and subsequent enforcement of compliance. Not every foyer is quite so strict, but they all have some form of vetting and this has been criticised as having "characteristics of the workhouse tests of the last century. This demanded servility in return for help, and weeded out the 'undeserving'".[18] The criticism is much overdone we would say.

One possible worry about foyers is that, on completion of training after 18 months to two years, the young people may feel reluctant to leave. Having made friends, they may not feel sanguine about finding a home for themselves. Even if they were given independent social housing, they might justifiably fear isolation. Some foyers are working hard to provide "move-on" and "after-care". Without this, much good work will be undone. Even with it, ensuring that young people who have gained skills and employment prospects can also maintain social and family relationships will also be essential if they are to use their new home as a springboard for a fulfilling job and social life.

Several foyers reported to us the difficulty of attracting young people from black and minority ethnic communities, particularly South Asians. As unemployment is disproportionately evident amongst racial minorities,[19] this is a concern that must be addressed if foyers are to fulfil their full purpose.

CHILDREN AND YOUNG PEOPLE

Many people expressed misgivings to us about the high number of single parents being housed by social landlords. Fifty-six per cent of new tenants in social housing with dependent children are now single parents[20] as we discuss in Chapter 3. There are also worries about the numbers of children in small flats and houses.

> Child density increases as does the wear and tear on the estate and so will litter, graffiti and subsequently vandalism; this in turn worsens the estate's reputation, produces a higher turnover and so the process feeds on itself. Excessively high numbers of children on an estate could therefore offer a possible mechanism through which the spiral of decline operates.[21]

Page is arguing above for a reduction in child densities. In some places they are already high and only a quarter of housing associations had initiated child care projects, though nine out of ten of these had tenants involved, suggesting that they were both popular and needed. Tenants were involved in starting up 27 per cent of child care projects. This was higher than the general figure for tenant initiation, which was 20 per cent, though still perhaps lower than one might have hoped. Seventeen per cent of child care activities had been going for more than five years, and 44 per cent had been established in the last two years. The Friendship Group in Birmingham has provided child care since the 1960s. They commented, "these services have always been targeted at single parent families, to assist with opportunities to take paid employment or training." Child care can have many side-benefits. Nurseries and primary schools bring people together as we discuss in Chapter 3. They are one of the most important meeting points in a neighbourhood and are often the wellspring of lifelong relationships, sometimes amongst the children, but certainly amongst the adults. The absence of decent child care keeps single parents at home, keeps them unemployed and keeps them poor.

We visited an estate in London built in the 1980s and bought "off the shelf" from a developer. All the tenants had been nominated by the local authority and there were a large proportion of single parents, many of whom had previously been homeless. It was by no means an ideal design for families with young children. Two children sleep in a small double bedroom. The estate has much redundant car parking, more than one space for each house, but no outdoor play space. Employment training had been linked with child care on the estate. A local college was setting aside training places, which sometimes could not be taken up at all unless children were looked after. The community development worker told us about one woman who had taken up a place at the college to do an electrical installation course before there was a crèche.

> Once she'd sorted out her childcare – she got a lot of support in finding minders and suitable child-care placements – got over that major hurdle – she thought why wasn't she doing this training before. She then wanted to do it full time. We helped her and she did an access course to do social work training.

Estate tenants have been trained in childcare in preparation for employment in the crèche, which will be part of the estate's community centre – itself designed by tenants and now being built by trainees some of whom come from the estate. Some of the problems of the estate stem from the fact that it was not built for its current purpose. The allocations to the estate seem more to have been driven by the need to get people out of temporary accommodation, a laudable enough motive, but not if the consequence is a community of multiple deprivation in unsuitable housing. Nonetheless, despite these unpropitious beginnings, the association and the tenants had made the best of the material, particularly the human capital, available to them. So one department of the association should be commended, even if the department that made the purchase and the lettings arrangements might usefully reconsider its approach before embarking on another similar venture.

Youth initiatives are more recent. No projects were running five years ago, and half of them had been initiated in the last year, prompted by concern about anti-social behaviour and the misery of youth unemployment. One of the most ambitious is the Youth Strategy Plan of the William Sutton Trust. This ranges from holiday play schemes to employment training for young people. The strategy emphasises multi-agency working and the need for "professional support, advice and guidance for tenants' groups who wish to develop activities and facilities for children and young people".

CREDIT UNIONS

Paradoxically, some of the places in Britain where the poorest people live, relying very often on state benefits, are also the most expensive. Shops and public transport are often more costly than in other communities. Worse still, the money that does come into the poorest communities leaves it faster. In the Newtown district of Birmingham money in the area only circulates between one or two people before it is exported from the local community. In middle-class areas, money can go through five or ten pairs of hands before leaving the community. Money flows through low-income communities "like water through sand" according to Pat Conaty, Development Director of the Aston Commission.[22] In addition, borrowing can be difficult and expensive. One thousand bank branches closed between 1989 and 1994. According to an unpublished study by the Bank of England[23] one in six of the wards in Birmingham no longer has a branch of a bank or a building society in it. In Greater Easterhouse in Glasgow one branch of a bank remains to serve a population of 40,000. Although many banks have closed because of electronic "hole-in-the-wall" and telephone banking, many local people on estates continue to harbour the suspicion that banks are reluctant to keep branches open in poor communities. If people do not have the money or the credit rating for banks to allow them to use cash cards, or debit or credit cards, when they do need money they have no alternative but to turn to informal lenders, sometimes charging extortionate rates of interest. In Newtown the Social Justice Commission heard of interest rates between 60 and 500 per cent.

Credit unions can be a community-owned outlet for saving and gaining credit at a reasonable interest rate. In Cranhill in Glasgow people save anything from £1 to £5 per week. Investors in the Winson Green Credit Union in Birmingham can borrow up to twice the amount paid in at an interest rate that is a fraction of that charged by private money lenders. Credit unions take a variety of forms, from those with millions of pounds of assets, high quality offices and paid staff to those entirely dependent on volunteers and with assets of less than £10,000.[24] They are a mechanism to save and secure fairly small loans, usually less than £10,000, for people who might have difficulty in gaining loans from conventional lenders. Community credit unions are most successful when grafted on to existing community organisations, avoiding the need to set up a new administrative structure, find new volunteers, appoint officers and so on.[25]

In the world at large credit unions are growing in popularity, particularly amongst poorer people, as part of the growth in micro-credit. In Canada, for example 40 per cent of the population belong to a credit union. One household in four is part of a credit union in Ireland.

The Indian sub-continent has been the fountainhead of the micro-credit movement. The writer Gita Mehta recounts an early endeavour in the field, "In the early fifties the poorest women in Ahmedabad," the capital of the Indian state of Gujarat, "pooled the meagre sums they earned by scavenging in refuse dumps, pulling hand carts, selling rags, breaking stones for roads, carrying bricks in cane baskets on their heads, and started their own co-operative bank. They called themselves S.E.W.A. (the acronym means *service* in Hindi) the Self-Employed Women's Association. Their bank enabled them to take out loans and invest in such things as a sewing machine to make garments to sell. As soon as one group's initial investment is returned, another group of women took out another loan to start a cottage industry and become economically secure." By 1997 S.E.W.A has branches all over India and has thirty thousand members.26 The Gramene Bank in Bangladesh is perhaps the best known example. It is a huge trust-based micro-credit project involving millions of people. Borrowers are asked to make a verbal agreement to repay the loan. A small group, no more than ten, of nearby members monitor the agreement. There is no penalty for default other than the breaking of trust between friends, relatives, neighbours and fellow citizens. More than 75 per cent of loans are repaid in full.

Only ten housing associations said they supported credit unions. All of these had started in the last five years, and some had not yet got fully going. One association had a credit union involving 197 tenants but they comment that, "the number and extent of tenant involvement has varied and is difficult to sustain." Credit unions need an effective administration. For this reason workplace-based credit unions, often with administrative support from the management, are growing four times faster than community credit unions, many of which are run by volunteers.

All housing association tenants have an account – the rent account – into which they pay or into which housing benefit is paid. The administrative role in credit unions could be played by social landlords who are now housing the poorest members of our society. People, particularly women, save even from meagre resources, but they do not always have access to ways of doing it efficiently and safely.

LOCAL EXCHANGE TRADING SCHEMES

Local Exchange Trading Schemes (LETS) rely on a separate "currency" which acts as a "supplement" to ordinary money. Services which could only be afforded by people in full-time paid work are obtainable locally through LETS. A directory of members is printed, listing what they offer and how much they charge or what they want. The usual practice is to charge an hourly rate in the local "currency". Services provided and received are recorded, and then traded. It is a form of multilateral mutual aid where the giver and the receivers do not have to swap directly; instead a whole circuit of people can be involved. The first formal LETS scheme started in Canada in 1983. They were then established in Australia and New Zealand. Only two housing associations in our survey are involved in LETS, despite their growing popularity in general. One of them, Liverpool Housing Trust, part-funds a unit to establish LETS and offers training to tenants on how to establish them.

We visited the Beckford LETS in Wiltshire. Most of the members live in social housing. Set up in 1995 originally for people with a history of mental health problems, the scheme aspired not just to relieve the poverty of living on benefits but also to ameliorate the isolation of living alongside often suspicious, sometimes hostile strangers. They adopted a slogan early: "Let's create a caring community we can be proud of." By 1997 it had 50 members, about a third of whom as it turned out had no history of mental health problems. Harry Turner, the originator, could not over-stress the importance of building a community before building an exchange network.

> We decided rather than have a situation where we were trying to promote LETS, we had a situation where we got together social meetings because one of the things we've discovered about developing an ordinary LETS is that the confidence to start using the scheme comes about when people get to know each other. We organised a ten week programme of different events – an introduction to massage, painting – this, that and the other. The first meeting we had was 'What is LETS' but the way we did it was informal. We had people from the existing LETS come and talk about how LETS had helped them and that worked brilliantly; it was the best start-up meeting I've ever been to. It turned into a deeply moving evening where people with mental health problems were exchanging ideas about who they were and what they wanted from the world.

Once the exchange trading scheme was established, a virtuous circle of contacts and activities was established. There is a strong social element, with complementary therapy sessions and weekly social engagements.

We end with a success story from an estate we visited in the North East of England. The centre could not hold. Things had fallen apart. "Social meltdown" was the phrase used by one of the tenants.

Widespread unemployment following the closure of major local employers and the poor state of the housing gave the place a bad reputation making it hard-to-let. Two blocks of flats had become virtually uninhabitable. People did not want to live in them. As they got transferred away, their flats were vandalised and gutted. Crime was rampant; rubbish was being tipped everywhere, dirty nappies were left lying around; cars were constantly driven across open spaces making it impossible for children to play. Nonetheless, some people were committed to the area and did not want to leave. A small nucleus of people turned themselves into a management co-operative and worked with architects to redevelop the two blocks. All went well. The new co-op took responsibility for allocations, caretaking and repairs. When the flats were re-occupied there was a mix of generations, single people, people with children. Co-op members themselves landscaped the areas around the block. After six months there had not been one break-in.

After this initial success, the co-op became more ambitious. With the help of a local housing association the co-op took over a derelict piece of land using their own labour to build houses and bungalows for co-op members to move into – people whose needs had changed but who did not want to leave the neighbourhood. They created 15 jobs for themselves. Most of them still have jobs in the building industry now.

So some of the foundations for building strong communities – stability of residence, several generations living together and a high level of mutual aid – have not just made a difference to the housing situation. Employment has been increased, albeit marginally, in an area with one of the highest unemployment rates in the country. Crime has diminished. Investment not just in buildings but also in people has been repaid in new economic activity as well as in savings on repairs and in the cost of crime.

* * *

The picture that emerges from our survey and case studies is that housing associations are committed to housing those in the greatest need, but some feel that this is enough (or more than enough) to ask. Others reacted to the new needs in a most positive way. They encourage tenants and residents' associations and increasingly provide buildings for them to meet in. This is all to the good. It brings people together. There is clear tenant interest in child care and some support from housing associations, but more is possible and desirable. Sharing child care, especially between the generations, creates bonds which can be lasting, as well as facilitating training and employment, particularly for single parents. Some housing associations also help old and disabled people to stay in their own homes, or near to them. A recent interest has been shown in assisting young people which is greatly to be welcomed.

Many of the key activities are in place. They need to be extended and built upon. The first purpose of the survey was to indicate the sort of community activities housing associations are promoting outside their traditional brief. We have shown that there is a wide range of them and that since 1993 there has been an acceleration in the numbers which have been taken up. The numbers and the vitality are greater than we had expected. All of the projects and activities add to the texture of mutuality in and around social housing. We hope that the trend will not be arrested, and that the initiatives of the associations will be drawn more closely into collaboration with the similar initiatives of local authorities.

The second purpose has been to give an impression of how far housing associations are giving local people the chance to help each other more fully. On that score we cannot come to such an optimistic conclusion. More effort seems to have gone into starting organisations than into associating tenants with them, as organisers, as volunteers, as well-wishers. Here is one deficiency that it should not be too painful to remedy.

chapter three

Building Blocks of Community

The last chapter was about formal organisations of the kind that communities need. Even more they need the informal. The most fundamental mutual aid is between individuals who may or may not be members of any body other than the family. But the informal, as we have pointed out, matters a great deal to the state. The welfare state has a vital and also a residual function. It does for people – rightly does for people – what they cannot do for themselves. But they can still do a great deal for themselves.

This has not often been recognised in the protracted debate on community which promises to come to a head by the turn of the century. Attention has recently centred on what should be done to transfer the financial costs from the taxpayer to individuals required to pay for old people's homes and the like. It has rarely, though there are some notable exceptions, centred on what should be the far more important matter of informal care, and how it can be maintained, or, indeed, increased. It is assumed that informal care has to be written into such calculations as a given: that the amount and quality of informal care cannot be influenced by what the state does; in short, that the informal cannot be encouraged by the formal. This is the belief so often taken for granted which this book does not take for granted at all. Our intention is to challenge the conventional view.

Informal care matters to many people other than the elderly. A great deal has been said, often with a bitter edge to it, about the "burden" of lone mothers on the state. Why do some of the 1.4 million go out to work and others not? It is far more because their children have the informal care of the grandparents than the formal care of crèches, nurseries and child minders. The formal is certainly needed but even more so the informal. It is broadly the same story with children who are "taken into care", as it is called. Care is given in children's homes or with foster or adoptive parents because the care they needed did not come from the family. Children who truant, or take up drugs, or take to vicious violence while still at primary school, or run so wild that they are the bane of police forces across the country are all suffering from the lack of the same informal care in the family, neighbours, friends and the socially-minded and generous-hearted in the community.[1]

Our national debt may be serious, but we argue that the national deficit in care is far more so. The demand for care is much greater than the supply, and the deficit needs to be met less by the extension of the welfare state in the form we have known it than by an extension of the informal system, or perhaps it would be better to say informal care should be admitted into a new welfare state. The informal, already the main provider of care, needs to do more. The job of the welfare state in the future, apart from its principal task of preventing poverty by redistributing resources from the rich to the poor, is to support and promote the informal. The unusual characteristic of housing we mentioned in Chapter 1, which it shares with education, is that the gross sum spent on it should always be converted into a net sum to allow for the consequent savings on health care, on community and social services, and law and order.

Sir Roy Griffiths in his report to the government on community care made the same point. He was unusual in proposing, as we are doing, that the function of the public services was to back up the great host of informal carers.

> Publicly provided services constitute only a small part of the total care provided to people in need. Families, friends and neighbours and other local people provide the majority of care in response to needs which they are uniquely well placed to identify and respond to. This will continue to be the primary means by which people are enabled to live normal lives in community settings.

The proposals [for community care services] take as their starting point that this is as it should be, and that the first task of publicly provided services is to support and where possible strengthen these networks of carers. Public services can help by identifying such actual and potential carers, and tailoring the provision of extra services (if required) accordingly.[2]

THE THREE GROWING POINTS OF COMMUNITY

The word community, while always referring to what people have in common, is employed in many different contexts. The most ordinary use is when community refers to place. It then refers to the people who live in a place or territory and, more than that, to people who have some bonds between them by reason of living there. The notion matters to our argument because such territorial communities are, when members provide for each other, the settings for much of the informal care whose value was estimated in Table 1 (Chapter 1, above). It follows from this point of view alone that if networks of carers are to be strengthened (in Griffiths' words), communities need to be too. It is almost, but not quite, a tautology.

But how to do it? First of all, the nature of such communities has to be understood. Unrelated people will not care for each other unless they feel a bond with others who live in that place. If they do, and share community spirit or community solidarity, they will ordinarily be ready to help each other.

If you go and live in a new place for a short time, as a transient you will be unusual if you develop any great attachment to the place or the people who live there. But stay there over a period of years and you will be equally unusual if you do not feel that to some extent you belong there. The place becomes part of your identity. Stability of residence makes for identity within a community. People who stay in Sefton or Swindon end up by feeling they belong to Sefton or Swindon, and have a bond of psychological and sociological significance with others who do the same. Encouraging stability of residence should be part of any social policy for the future and the extension of teleworking should make it more economic.

Stable residence is the first key. A powerful second element is added if the residence becomes multi-generational. Children are the vital seedbed of community. As babies they are links to all other women and men who are mothers or fathers. Though so tiny, babies embody a sense of hope for the future of the community. Mothers and fathers have something in common just because they have children. In practice it may not mean much; but it can also mean a great deal. When they are a little older they are often more sociable than their parents and if they have the chance to meet with other children, at nursery or school, or if they can play with each other anywhere, they easily form friendships. They can then bring their parents together, often one of the strongest ties in a community.

The "school run", in or out of a car, is a common form of mutual aid, bringing together people, mostly women though increasingly men, to deliver children to one of the principal centres of community life almost everywhere, the primary school. On the Shipfield estate in Norfolk, which we visited, the taking of children to and from school creates an important bond between young single parents, many of whom are recent arrivals into a well-established community – some people have lived there for 30 years. One might fear, in that context, that the newly arrived single parents would feel isolated, excluded, possibly even ostracised as they do in so many other places; not so, however, and the school run is one reason why not.

Everywhere, the nursery or the primary school can be more than a school. It is a meeting place where people greet old friends and make new ones and, because the children have become friends, there is something of an obligation on even the most shy parents to become tolerably sociable towards other parents. As most of the children at a primary school live fairly close, once they become friends, the parents do not have far to go to see one another, as well as to pick up and deliver children. Older children can be more relied on to make their own way to school. So the need for parental supervision no longer exists and the daily contact between parents ends. But by the time the children reach secondary school age, the parents may have become friends in their own right, as was described to us on several of our visits.[3]

Eating and drinking together in the home or elsewhere has, from time immemorial, been the circumstance in which people find it easy to open up, relax, talk or just feel at ease with each other. Plato and St Benedict were early exponents of the social value of hospitality and eating together. So the parents of our older children who no longer meet at the school gates may meet, as at Shipfield, for "soup and salad suppers" or in a healthy eating club at the tenants' hall, and that will be another powerful reinforcement. In other countries sociable eating has become the central fact of some social housing.

ADDING KIN TO KITH

The third element is when kin is added to kith. If a parent has several children and they too stay in the same place, a local kinship group is in the making. When and if the children become parents, often forming relationships with someone nearby in their turn, a further and even more important strand is added to the web of human ties turning neighbours and friends into family in due course – uncles, aunts, cousins and grandparents.

Such an array of relatives serves several purposes. People can choose from amongst their relatives those they like being with for different reasons and find substitutes if their own parents let them down or, worst of all, abuse them. Each relative is also a link with further relatives and with their relatives' friends who are links into other kinship groups. The resulting close-knit network has a special kind of solidarity which comes from all or many of the members knowing each other. In this it is very different from a network unique to an individual. You may have many friends but the friends do not necessarily know each other. In a local kinship network or a series of them, all (or most) of the people in them also know each other. They feel themselves to be "members" of a kinship group and a community.

We know it was a long time ago but in the 1950s one of us in a partnership of two described how such a local kinship and community system provided informal care on a large scale.[4] Extended families constantly exchanged mutual aid, especially between women. A new parent could rely on her mother to act as the organiser of the social life and to look after the house and the other children while the wife was away in hospital having another baby, and to give advice which was specially valued because it came from someone who was so much part of one's life and at the same time so much more experienced.

> I take more notice of my Mum than I do of the welfare. She's had eight and we're all right. Experience speaks for itself, doesn't it?

That was on the big occasions. But there was a constant flow backwards and forwards on the smaller occasions as well. One consequence was that older people were by and large looked after by their children and grandchildren. The community was not just a set of relationships; it was also a moral economy, where goodness was exchanged in the form of help and support.

SURVIVAL OF KINSHIP

A long time ago? Yes, and it would not be worth mentioning unless such bonds are still of the utmost social importance. In a repeat survey which is in the course of being made in East London, but not yet published, despite all the changes, including the increase in the numbers of women who "go out" to paid work, mutual aid has emerged as still very marked, in and out of families, and in and out of the ethnic minorities, about which we will say more later in this chapter, as well as of the white populations. This is, for instance, shown by the extent to which grandparents are relied on by working mothers, and by non-working mothers for that matter when they need to nominate someone who will step in to act for them. Parents are required to give to the school their children attend the name of a proxy for themselves, so that if they are not available to come to the school in an emergency – as might happen when there is an accident, a child taken ill or exhibiting extreme bad behaviour – that someone can be asked to come right away to the school. In one particular primary school in East London in 1997, 243 families had one or more children at the school. As many as 181 of these gave grandparents as their emergency contacts, 148 of these were grandmothers (93 maternal, 37 paternal, 18 not stated), 33 grandfathers (17 maternal, 10 paternal and six not stated).

There are plenty of strong hints about the continuing importance of the extended family. The most recent survey of British social attitudes (1995) concluded that "the family is still the dominant source of support and care for most people".[5] A national survey by the Henley Centre found that amongst adults with mothers alive, 53 per cent had one living within five miles and of those who had a grandmother alive 47 per cent had one within the same five-mile radius. Over the years there have been other pointers as well:

1980: among 2,400 mothers who had recently had a baby, who went back to work and whose babies were cared for by someone else, it was usually a grandmother who took over.[6]

1987: two thirds of people asked whom they would "first look to for help" (excluding doctors) if a child "had a fairly serious illness", cited relatives with mothers and mothers-in-law being dominant.[7]

1994: where children were regularly looked after by grandparents, mothers chose them (for 76 per cent of children) because they thought that the children would be safe, secure and well looked after by them. Proximity of a mother's and grandmother's homes was a great boon to shared care between the generations.[8]

1994: 69 per cent of children between birth and 4 years old are looked after by relatives while their mother is at work. For five to 11 year olds, 57 per cent are looked after by relatives and 62 per cent of all children. Only 25 per cent of under 4s are looked after by a childminder and only 14 per cent go some of the time to a nursery. For five to 11 year olds, 23 per cent are looked after by friends and neighbours after school and during the holiday. The vast bulk of childcare support to working mothers is provided by family members.[9]

1995: After spouses' and partners' children, parents and siblings were most likely to be turned to for help with household jobs, assistance when ill and borrowing money.[10]

1995: 70 per cent of people agreed with the statement that people should keep in touch with close family members even if they don't have much in common. Fifty-five per cent of people agreed that people should keep in touch with relatives like aunts, uncles and cousins even if they don't have much in common. Seventy-two per cent of people strongly disagreed with the statement once children have left home they should no longer expect help from their parents.[11]

1995: 31 per cent of adults live less than 15 minutes' journey from their mother and a further 34 per cent would take less than an hour to reach their mother. Twenty-eight per cent could reach their father in 15 minutes and for a further 30 per cent it would take less than an hour. Sixty per cent of adults live less than an hour away from a brother or sister and 67 per cent within an hour of an adult child.[12]

1995: 48 per cent of adults see their mother at least once a week and a further 21 per cent at least once a month. The figures are similar for fathers. Fifty-eight per cent of adults see an adult child at least once a week and a further 16 per cent at least once a month.[13]

1997: of 1,000 children between 8 and 15, 78 per cent said that grandparents were key figures in their lives.[14]

THE VERTICAL FAMILY

There are two points we would like to stress from these surveys. The first is that the "vertical" family – the three-generational family – appears to be in quite a healthy state. It is the context for the new "lateral" family – the family of parents and children. Commentators never tire of gloomily reporting the weakening of the sense of family on the eve of its collapse, citing the increasing numbers of divorces and separations and the numbers of children who are not brought up by both their natural parents until they reach maturity, or at any rate leave school. These predictions of an imminent end to the family as we know it have been made more or less constantly since the industrial revolution. What the commentators do not so often say is that the vertical family does not seem to have weakened in the same way or to the same extent. The three-generational family appears to have survived relatively well. Perhaps the weakening of the lateral family has even strengthened the vertical family because the support of grandparents is even more important in the absence of a partner.

PROXIMITY

The other point we would like to make is about proximity: grandparents are not by any means always cut off from their grandchildren by distance. Even if they are geographically distant, they can still be brought together by means of the telephone and the car. BT and every other telephone company in the world would have to contract drastically if for some reason relatives stopped ringing each other. "Friends and Family" has become a BT marketing strategy. High technology monitoring systems have revealed the unsurprising fact that most private calls are made to friends and family and the telephone companies would very much like it if we made more.

The automobile industry would decline pretty rapidly if cars stopped being extended family transport. Where are all the millions of parents with children tied into the back seats speeding to at the weekend? Most of them are rushing to get to Grannie's, and in all the rush, managing to apologise over the mobile for being late. There are also many millions who cannot get to Grannie's by car. At the latest count only 29 per cent of housing association households had a car and 35 per cent of local authority tenants.[15] So for many social housing tenants, distant grandparents and no car generates a great cost in isolation and hardship faced alone.

Cars or no cars, phones or no phones, physical distance can be socially and psychologically distancing. The relationship is liable to be different when the same child can only see the older adult when brought there by the parents. A common type of relationship described by anthropologists the world over has been called "the merging of alternate generations". The tie between parents and children is one from which discipline, and the authority and obedience that discipline requires, cannot be fully removed, nor should it. But grandparents do not need to be in that same kind of way authority figures. They can show affection and love without them being combined with discipline. They can be more lenient. They can be more like friends. They can be more like children, and loved as a sort of a model of an adult which is different to that of the parents. This relationship brings more freedom for both the young person and the old one. Many parents marvel at the tolerance of grandparents; a tolerance, they say, that was not shown to them long ago by the selfsame people. But all that variety and fun can be a bit muted if whenever the grandparents and grandchildren are together, the parents are sitting there as well, watching.

Proximity matters because without it neither the grandchildren nor the grandparents can make their way to the other, unaccompanied, beyond a certain distance. If without a car, they cannot be near enough at hand to take the children to school in the morning or fetch them from school in the afternoon if the mother is not back from her work by then. The standard closing time of infant schools is 3pm and 3.30pm for primary schools.

Still more important is the tight timetable of most working mothers. To dovetail the daily arrangements with each other they have to be finely programmed even when there are cars in both generations. We know of one mother who gets into the car outside on the dot of five to eight every morning. She starts the engine of the car at the moment she sees the grandmother in her car come round the corner and into her street. They wave to each other like one Olympic runner handing the baton to another as the one shuttles past the other. The child is never left alone for more than a minute or so and the mother is in earshot almost until the grandmother is. But it is much more difficult to achieve synchrony if the grandparent has no car and the child has to be dropped and collected by a parent at the grandparent's house half an hour's drive away. The mother has to phone the grandparent in the afternoon to see if the alternate generations will still be in at the usual collection time. Then she will make the same run in reverse, taking at least as long as it did in the morning, provided that the traffic is no worse than usual. Sensitivity to the clock is very much at a premium. Without that gift, the whole bustling network can be brought down into disorder. How much easier, though, if the three generations live fairly close to each other, preferably within walking distance that is also safe. A facsimile of these arrangements can be simulated where the care of the child is entrusted to a paid carer, either a nanny who comes to the home or a childminder to whom the child is delivered. But this comes expensive and there is little evidence that parents prefer the care offered by paid carers to that offered by family members. The nanny or the child-minder may be as geographically proximate as a grandparent, but would they be as emotionally close? The motives for preferring care from within the family are not just financial. This is, if anything, even more so if the direction of care is the other way round and it is a more infirm grandparent who needs to receive rather than give. His or her need for assistance is not to the same extent capable of being routinised by the clock.

ETHNIC MINORITY COMMUNITIES

Proximity to family has also mattered greatly since the war, and continues to matter, to new arrivals in Britain from ethnic minorities. They may have few contacts and no job but very often the newly arrived migrant has a thread connecting them to family members from home now living here. Many black and minority ethnic people have worked hard and become more prosperous since they came, but few started with much save for their wits and their hard work. For these communities, particularly in their poorer times, some of the ties and bonds we have been discussing – family, proximity and stable residence and the mutual aid thereby engendered -have been the fundament of lightening the load of migration and explaining the enigma of arrival. Fifty years after the first migrations from the colonies and ex-colonies, although some of these ties have been eroded as they have in all communities, they are still evident.

To take the Caribbean community as an example: 550,000 people in Britain have their family origins in the Caribbean. But they are not a homogeneous community. People came from Jamaica, Barbados, Guyana, Trinidad, the Leeward Islands of Antigua, St

Kitts, Nevis, Montserrat and Anguilla, and from the Windward Islands of Dominica, Grenada, St Lucia and St Vincent. In Barbados the recruitment activities of British Rail, London Transport and the National Health Service acted as a magnet, but for the vast majority of people who left the Caribbean "family and island social networks were by far the most important channel of diffusing information and arranging initial footholds in Britain".[16]

After the evocatively named ship Empire Windrush brought the first wave of post-war Caribbean migrants in 1948 "chain migration" began. New arrivals, who were generally family and friends from home, were drawn to Britain and settled near those already here who might provide help with housing, finance and getting a job. People from St Vincent, for example, had a notable concentration in High Wycombe and those from Nevis in Leicester. In London, Jamaicans were particularly drawn to living south of the river, with Brixton as a focus, while Leeward and Windward islanders reproduced a kind of archipelago of concentrations north of the river – Dominicans around Paddington, Montserratians around Finsbury Park and so on. So proximity of family members was quickly re-asserted and although a significant minority of Caribbean people have moved away from these traditional areas of settlement to the suburbs, sometimes in order to get social housing, strong vestiges of that early proximity remain and were clearly discernible in answers to the 1991 census question about place of birth.[17] This early one to one reciprocal mutual aid offered to nearby new arrivals eventually became multilateral on a much larger scale. After a while food shops began to open, churches were formed, again very often reflecting island communities, community groups began to be established and, in the 1980s, black housing associations came into being.

All of these community groups ask people to become involved in contributing to the welfare of "our own people". There is an element of voluntary giving by those that can alongside offering help to those who need it, who may be the ones that help at other times. Research in 1996 commented, "many black associations had access to a wide network in the community including voluntary and self-help groups, churches and religious groups and neighbourhood fora. We found much less evidence of such extensive contacts at the mainstream housing associations we surveyed."[18] The Church of God in Christ, a pentecostal church in North London, has become the nucleus of a thriving credit union involving hundreds of members of the Church and their families, the level of trust and shared obligation creating a sense that money is safely invested and well looked after.

The same patterns of settlement, proximity, poorly paid work, community meeting places and, in the second generation, a degree of "suburbanisation" has taken place in the Indian community. For the Pakistani and Bangladeshi communities, there has been very little movement to the suburbs, partly because they are more recent arrivals without an adult British-born generation yet and partly because of poverty and unemployment. Pakistanis for example, often live in the same street in Bradford as relatives from their village in Pakistan. Bangladeshis in Tower Hamlets too have repeated patterns of proximate settlement of extended families. The only ethnic minority community to have significantly geographically dispersed is the Chinese community. Even for Chinese people there are significant concentrations in London and Manchester, often of people of Chinese ethnic origin, but who did not originate from mainland China, coming from Hong Kong, Malaysia or elsewhere. These places of origin are still reflected in places of settlement.

For all these communities into the second and third generations (and beyond in places of early settlement for black and ethnic minority people such as Bristol and Liverpool), ethnicity and culture continues to tie people together in family, neighbourhood and community. Mutual aid, not market economics, is the fuel that drives these constantly renewed contacts and commitments.

A pervasive belief about some ethnic minorities is that they have extended family living arrangements. But the 1991 census showed that even in ethnic minority communities the incidence of one household containing many families is reducing through the generations. What ordinarily has to be ruled out for all ethnic groups is that the three or four generation co-operative should live together under one roof. There is still a good deal of truth in the summing up of another study by Dr Sheldon in Wolverhampton, whose findings were very similar to those in Bethnal Green. He was speaking about older people.

> Both the old people and their younger relatives are agreed on the layout most suitable for many families which can be summed up as one of independent propinquity in separate establishments sited reasonably close to each other, so combining the advantage of independence and ready mutual aid. The movement away

of the younger generation inevitably leaves more old people who can no longer depend on the ready accessibility of their children; but it is essential to recognise this aspect of the natural history of old age and to assert a desire of the two generations to live closer to each other, for otherwise we are depriving ourselves of what has hitherto been one of the principal methods by which so many families have elected to care for their old people.[19]

We are in danger of continuing and adding to that deprivation if we carry on as we have carried on since the 1950s. Mobility has increased and will continue to do so and not just in the towns and cities. As a Cheshire respondent to the Rural Development Commission's 1994 *Lifestyles in Rural England* survey commented, "Those coming in are wealthier. Our daughters will not be able to live locally unless new starter homes are built."[20] The labour and housing markets currently seem to demand mobility, but for the future home and teleworking may yet change all that. Even so, kinship cannot again bulk as large in society as it did when George Lansbury was a child or even as when the Bethnal Green studies were made in the 1950s. Other means of providing mutual aid have to be found to supplement the many services which families can still provide.

Community is the larger, more all-embracing concept. It is rather like seeds which once sown in the soil take a long time for the trees to grow to their full height. Stability of residence (as we have been saying) creates community and the resulting community can have many groupings within it, including kinship. Kinship groupings grow naturally within and just like the communities of which they are part. Yet even if kinship can never again be as central as it once was, it is still one of the sinews of society to be encouraged by housing policy, not weakened as it has been so far. And communities also encourage close relations between neighbours and all sorts of people who meet and like each other (or the opposite) without there being any kinship tie between them. Communities make friendships and, although friends do not ordinarily have such a strong sense of duty towards each other as relatives, friendship is for some people, especially for young adults, as much the essence of their society as kinship. Communities of friendship, communities of interest and communities of adversity and the mutual aid they engender are discussed further in Chapter 5.

The "speaking for" system

East London was certainly not typical – nor could it or any other place be that – of working-class districts. But there is no reason to think that the methods by which housing was allocated in the early days of the welfare state were so very different from those in use elsewhere over the length and breadth of the country. As one of us has described elsewhere,[21] for working-class people private housing was the norm, with rents under the stringent control of the Rent Restriction Acts. The landlords were extremely remiss in carrying out repairs. They claimed the low rents gave them no margin. Often they were right. But by and large they were certainly no Rachmans like those who flourished where properties were worth a great deal more and let to newcomers in very urgent need of housing with few local ties. The general system for the poor exemplified the value which David Hume, the great Scottish philosopher, placed on propinquity as one of the ties which made isolated human beings into fellows one of another.

This system meant that working-class women, and particularly the Mums, had a valuable property right. Different landlords in a district often employed the same rent collectors and the rent collectors chose who should get a new tenancy when someone died or moved elsewhere while on this earth. The rent collectors wanted to be as sure as they could that the new tenants were reliable payers, and the best oracle of that was the mother's record. Controlled private ownership played right into the kinship network and was its most powerful support, ensuring that on the whole married daughters and many married sons lived where they wanted to, close to their mothers and fathers and their other relatives.

"Speaking for" worked simply and personally. When one of her daughters was going to get married, the mother made it her business to get to know about all the impending vacancies. She was, naturally, more likely to know about people moving out, or planning to move out, near to her own home. Not only was her knowledge more complete, her influence with the landlord and rent collector in her district was also greater. Mrs Robbins, who lived in the same street with her mother and five married sisters, explained the process at its simplest.

> My mother has lived here for years and my sisters were all living here. We knew the collector and spoke to him. That's how we got the place.

It could be a lifelong tenancy which could even be for more than one life, being heritable by children who lived at home, a principle of succession that now applies to social housing tenancies too.

The housing trusts which managed the blocks of tenement buildings followed suit until the 1980s. The Nags Head Housing Society ruled "that only children or other relatives should be entitled to vacancies". The local superintendent of another justified the policy.

> We prefer sons and daughters. They know all the rules through having lived here. They know what has to be done. You don't get no trouble with them.

"Speaking for" accounted for the extreme localisation of kin. In one street in Bethnal Green containing 59 households, 28 had relatives in it; in one block of buildings containing 52 households, 28 had relatives in it; in another block, with 176 households, 64 had relatives. "Speaking for" also reinforced the dominance of Mum in her family as owner-occupied property has enhanced the dominance of men.

THE GREAT SWITCH OF TENURE

After the Second World War began the long-drawn out clearance of slums, of the cosy but often dilapidated cottages which had survived. But it was not just slums that were to be cleared. With them went "the honeyed squalor of home", as Laurie Lee called it. So there had to be a new way of deciding who got what. The whole informal, intimate and chancy network of relatives "speaking for" relatives held sway only up to the doors of the town hall. Inside, "speaking for" was no time-hallowed custom. Even if it had lasted for a long time it was not hallowed, it was nepotism. Fraternity had to be ushered out and Equality ushered in. The "speaking for" system was partly abolished and the reign of the housing waiting list was established, with people being given new dwellings according to their need, not judged by their social need to be close to their support network of people but according to their physical housing need for shelter or for more or different space.

For three kinds of service which were fundamental to human well-being – housing as well as health and education – the list was formed on the principle, Who is in the greatest need? Distribution of the new housing was according to one sort of need – "housing need". People in the "worst" housing, judged by criteria like over-crowding on the part of parents and their children, sickness and disability, lack of water supply or indoor lavatory and bath, were henceforth to get priority. There was great variety in the detail of how the new egalitarian housing policy was administered. But in almost all the schemes endlessly worked over and re-worked by local housing committees, priority was graded according to the number of points awarded to applicants for different components of housing need. The waiting list was born similar to the one which rules the health service. Rationing has worked through making people wait. Thus were the central queues of society created. The need to meet need is accepted, but subject to systematic postponement.

It is hardly ever the case that when one tradition-to-be is installed, another tradition-that-was is completely overthrown. Nepotism was not completely banished. There was always family pressure on councils from voters as there is now and always will be as long as families survive. Neither local parents nor their local children could see why, when they married, housing administrators had to turn away children who were as keen to live in the community where they had been born and bred as the parents were keen to have them there. They were keen partly for the sake of the exchanges of help and support, sometimes tempered by frustration or occasional-ly worse, which are the bread and butter of most extended families.

Why should strangers with more points but no affection for each other be brought in to occupy a house which would be ideal for their children? The councillors plagued with the question had children themselves. They could see the point as well as the points. But although they had to struggle to find different answers, they often compromised a little towards Fraternity against the imperatives of Equality, so that preference for sons and daughters did not quite die out for some decades to come.

The unfolding of a crisis

Television has had a part in the story. The screening of the drama-documentary *Cathy Come Home* in 1966, charting how one family had lurched from disadvantage and poverty into home-lessness, awoke public concern to a phenomenon the public knew little of at the time: despite the millions of new council homes built since 1945 many young parents and their children still had nowhere to live.

By coincidence, within a few days of the showing of the film Shelter was established. The film gave its campaign against homelessness direction and purpose. The new organisation had staff, an infrastructure, plenty of energy and tactical grip. After many years, the result of this campaign was the Homeless Persons Act 1977. The legislation ensured that Cathy and those like her would for the first time have some assurance of being given a high priority for council housing, even though she would not necessarily be housed straight-away. Homelessness carried people to the top of the waiting list.

The new law was effective. In 1979 councils accepted 70,038 households as homeless. This figure rose annually and reached a peak in 1991 of 178,867. By 1995 it had fallen to 134,501.[22] It is doubtful whether the actual number of people becoming homeless grew in this way. What changed was the obligation put on councils to house them and the determination of homeless families and their advocates that the obligation should be honoured. The rehoused once-homeless families often began the process of engagement with an unfamiliar community with precious few resources and trying to get through doors not always open or welcoming to strangers.

Homeless families were not the only component of increasing demand for social housing. The rate of household formation began to grow in the late 1960s. The availability of a large new supply of council housing encouraged people who would previously have gone on living together, often in conditions that we would now regard as overcrowded or lacking amenities, into splitting off and forming new households, fulfilling the prediction of Sheldon that we quoted earlier in this chapter. This has also happened outside social housing: a growth in people's wish to live on their own – 4 per cent lived on their own in 1961, now it is 12 per cent[23] – and in bigger spaces, and with it has grown the demand for all kinds of housing in all sectors. To keep pace it is projected that about 200,000 homes a year will be needed every year for the next ten years in England alone, and, as we have said, about half of those will need to be social housing for rent. These changes were not too socially destructive so long as these new households lived near enough to sustain pre-existing arrangements of mutuality – grandparents and neighbours offering help with childcare and adult children, often supported by other people nearby, caring for their elderly relatives and friends, maintaining proximity in the way we have already discussed. However, the allocation of social housing made sure that in many places they did not end up living sufficiently close together to sustain these relationships.

RACE RELATIONS ACT 1976

Over almost exactly the same period of the late 1970s and early 1980s another consideration came into play, following the passage of the Race Relations Act 1976. Unfair results from the allocation of social housing had long been suspected: black and ethnic minority people having to wait longer for social housing and in many instances getting housing of inferior quality. These were not simply the outcomes of prejudice on the part of the allocators. Other aspects of the prioritising system put black people and members of other ethnic groups at a disadvantage with no necessary malice aforethought on the part of any individual housing allocator. Inquiries by the Commission for Racial Equality into the policies of Hackney,[24] Tower Hamlets[25] and elsewhere confirmed these suspicions.

Firstly, there was the requirement to have lived in an area for some years before being considered eligible for the waiting list – the residential qualification. Refugees and other new arrivals were thus put at a considerable disadvantage. The Asians expelled from East Africa in the 1970s were a case in point. Many were forced to purchase old rundown property which they could ill afford and live very overcrowded because they did not meet the residential requirement and so were not eligible for social housing.[26]

Secondly, the treatment of separated families was indirectly discriminatory. In investigating the allocations policies of the London Borough of Tower Hamlets, the Commission for Racial Equality found that families separated within the UK were offered housing big enough to allow the family to re-unite, but when part of the family was abroad, housing would be offered only for the section of the family that was already in the UK, often a single man. Only when the whole family arrived were they eligible for large enough housing for them all. As many Bangladeshi families were relatively large, when they did arrive in Tower Hamlets and elsewhere there was no large enough council housing available. If they could not stay with relatives, they spent two years or more in temporary housing, often in seedy bed and breakfasts far from relatives, friends and community across the other side of London. Much of this hardship could have been avoided if families divided between countries could have been treated in the same way as families separated within Britain. There would still have been a wait, but not one spent in demoralising temporary housing long enough to put down shallow roots in the stony soil of an unfamiliar neighbourhood before being uprooted once more when a council or a housing association home became available.

Finally, and most importantly, the priority given to sons and daughters of existing tenants, often in preference to the homeless or overcrowded people, meant that all white neighbourhoods could remain white. For example, on the Isle of Dogs black families, who were more likely to be homeless, had to wait longer and often ended up with worse quality property than relatively less needy white applicants who had the advantage of having parents who were already council tenants, if indeed black people got housed on the Island at all. Black families had not been in Britain long enough to have adult children so the benefits of the sons and daughters policy did not fall to them, just its disadvantage – people from far away were less likely to get housed quickly.

As a result of these persistent findings, one by one local authorities in multi-racial neighbourhoods removed residential requirements and struck out the priority given to sons and daughters, often willingly in a political climate that valued equality of opportunity and the need to ration social housing more fairly. The vestiges of the old "speaking for" system were no more. Housing departments, housing associations and housing trusts, even the Crown for its property, moved over generally to a system of priority for people who were homeless, in palpably insecure accommodation or very overcrowded.

So increased demand for social housing and a re-ordering of priorities in search of a new sort of equality, racial equality, which had not much figured before, both important in themselves, removed the emphasis that had hitherto been placed on existing relationships of kinship and mutuality. The result was inevitable. The priority offered to some of those who were not homeless was removed and sons and daughters of existing tenants now took their place a long way behind Cathy in the queue, unless they too could demonstrate that they were homeless. Even if they managed to do that, there was no guarantee that they would be housed near their parents or siblings. One of our growth points for community – proximity – had been comprehensively undermined.

The consequences were felt in rural as well as urban areas, where some of the same forces were at work, if not for the same reasons. It may not have been the case that local authorities in rural areas wanted to ensure fairness to ethnic minorities, but the distancing and dispersal of family members continued and continues as the commitment to keeping families living near to one another was eroded and the availability of social or other forms of cheap housing diminished. One respondent from Wiltshire told the Rural Development Commission's *Lifestyles* survey,

> It seems unsatisfactory that young people are almost forced away to housing estates where they are cut off somewhat and cut off from the family. The whole idea of the family in its supportive role is lost. In turn, the children are not around to support the parents in old age.[27]

PRIORITY NEED OR BALANCED COMMUNITIES

The picture of who actually gets social housing is always more complex and varied than the beguilingly satisfying notion of a fair queue of people in priority need, benignly waiting their turn and giving way, if necessary, to people who asked for housing more recently than them but were deemed to be in greater need.

In practice, there are many exceptions to this general rule. One is the system for dealing with places which are "hard to let". The problem of hard to let social homes was discussed as early as 1968. Anne Power describes these events,

> Government officials were shocked to see lettings advertisements in property pages for government-funded tower blocks after 1968, in spite of allegedly long queues of slum clearance families waiting to be rehoused. The whole idea of government housing was that it would meet almost infinite demand from otherwise excluded groups. There were shock waves amongst British decision-makers when it became clear that some slum clearance areas were wrongly designated and that people preferred them to a brand new flat. The case of Barnsbury in London was the most celebrated (Ferris, 1972). There, slum clearance plans dating from the 1930s were abandoned in 1969 in favour of area improvement, as long-standing tenants refused to be moved. Many people, even in fairly dire conditions, simply would not accept rehousing in tower blocks after Ronan Point.[28]

In 1996 housing associations identified 40,000 homes in over

500 estates that they were finding hard to let. Although the overall proportion of difficult to let stock may appear to be small, almost two thirds of the associations involved in the research study managed stock they saw as difficult to let.[29] Other studies of the current situation have shown that, in fact, there are two systems of allocation. For places where people want to live there is a queue based on need. For places where people do not want to live, there are far fewer restrictions.[30] One housing association reported that a series of advertisements in local papers of vacancies on a large ex-local authority estate produced 300 enquiries. All applicants were interviewed and by the end of 1996 the association had filled more than 100 empty homes on the estate and many others on other estates. Over 65 per cent of these new tenants were in employment with most earning reasonably high wages. The majority had no children, so on traditional housing needs criteria they would have been unlikely to get a look-in for this or any other social housing. The association now has a waiting list for the once unpopular estate and there has been a welcome side-benefit in reducing rent arrears. The association has extended this policy to two other difficult to let estates.[31]

Housing for people with special needs has always screened out those who are felt by professionals to lack the necessary independence, sometimes to the point that it is hard to discern the exact nature of the "special" need. This has led some to note that there are rather more vulnerable people in "general needs housing" than there are in "special needs housing". Whether or not the former receive any support from the landlord is sometimes a chancy business.[32] Foyers too exclude those who are thought to lack the motivation to stick to the training programme. So, it is not those in "priority need" for employment who get the benefits of life in a foyer; it is those thought most able to benefit. They are unlikely to be the ones in greatest need.

We visited a new housing association estate in a semi-rural location in the Midlands. The land had been given free to the housing association on condition that it be used to provide social housing for local people; this was in an area with a shortage of affordable housing and pressure on house prices from commuters and incomers. The District Council had 100 per cent nominations to the new tenancies and everyone had either to live, work or have family in the town. The first tenants mostly came from other housing in the town and were on the waiting or transfer lists, but not necessarily in urgent need. This did not mean that those in need lost out as all the local families on the waiting list at the time were housed. In an area of admittedly lower housing stress these arrangements were more viable. We found a quiet community where people living on the estate were well integrated into the town through their existing links and activities. They did not feel the need for a strong community focus or facilities on the estate because they were so near the town and their existing networks. We have talked of building communities on estates, but for social housing which is not built as an estate in areas where tenure is mixed, the town, as in the above example, may be the focus of the community. With this in mind the wisdom of building peripheral estates has been rightly re-considered. Emphasis must be also be placed on integrating social housing tenants with others in schools, churches and other community meeting places on and off estates. Finally the degradation of town centres and the preference for out of town development, particularly for shopping, will need to be reversed. The denuding of town centres of social and commercial life bears much harder on the poor and the old, with far fewer cars amongst them.

So the absolute importance of housing people in the greatest need straightaway – a very fine principle indeed – is in practice quite often undermined in a big way by practical considerations and in numerous small ways, only some of which have been mentioned above. All in all, however, housing policy has augmented the other changes which were afoot to break up families on a large scale. The slums were cleared and the communities that were there were sometimes preserved in the new housing, but very often they were dispersed. The people at the top of the waiting list, often the most vulnerable, poor and desperate, were rehoused wherever dwellings became vacant even though they were far from where they wanted to be, and where they might have received support. The nation moved further into an age where services which had once been rendered informally as part of the basic lore and custom of life were performed by agents of the same welfare state which with a different rule book separated so many people from so many people.

Since the Page reports which we have already cited another criticism of social housing has been voiced: that it is not producing "balanced" communities. New people moving in should (it is now said) be mixed with existing tenants and transfers from other estates or properties known to the landlord. One "balance" lies between people who are homeless and/or unemployed and those who have been in social housing rather longer. The poor are thus mixed with the poorest. There is no necessary balance between age groups and certainly no balance which reflects the range of social-economic groups in society as a whole. Social layering and segregation is only very slightly ameliorated. The middle class are notable by their absence. Nor are there many people who have been resident in the neighbourhood for a long time who might know each other well and are aware of the bonds of mutuality. Nor does it guarantee the spread of ages and generations. None of our growth points of community will necessarily be achieved.

Nonetheless, having a mixed or balanced community has a commonsense appeal and has given rise to some experiments in "community lettings". In our survey, which we discussed in detail in Chapter 2, 34 per cent of responding housing associations said that they sought to use their allocations systems to achieve a social and economic mix and 40 specific projects were mentioned with this as an objective. Many commented on feeling constrained by the local authority's allocations procedures and the Housing Corporation's regulatory requirements. There is however a growing feeling, particularly on estates which are difficult to let or difficult to manage, that the sensitive management of allocations may beneficially affect the life of the community, and indeed the life of the housing manager. These "community lettings" arrangements have been introduced with various motives in mind mostly to do with reducing or preventing anti-social behaviour, a proxy, perhaps, for community-building but a limited and negative one. There has not yet been any systematic evaluation of such lettings schemes. Preliminary indicators are somewhat equivocal.

> Allocations policies do have a role to play in improving
> and maintaining the quality of life on housing estates,
> but their contribution should not be exaggerated.[33]

It is unlikely that, without a clearer objective about what makes up a successful community of the sort we have described, any tinkering with allocations priorities will have a very significant long-term impact, except in very particular circumstances. On an estate we visited in a poor part of the North of England – now afflicted by unacceptably high structural unemployment – crime had reached epidemic proportions, so much so that the tenants contrived never to leave their homes empty. An aggressive campaign by the police and the landlord, prosecuting and evicting trouble makers wherever possible, combined with a sensitive approach to new lettings has in the view of the tenants put things back on an even keel. Perhaps if a different approach had been taken to allocations in the first place and steps taken to ensure that people moving in did feel in some way bound to other people in the place, sharing some sense, however attenuated, of collective responsibility, the problem would not have got so serious.

As a result of everything that has happened, priority housing need has been defined in increasingly narrow ways. Little attention has been given to length of residence in a neighbourhood, ties of kinship or friendship, the spread of ages or generations, or the need for, or the ability to give, support to someone else in the community. Little wonder then that people who know not much about one another and feel no particular bond towards others nearby should also sometimes be the people who are casually destructive of other people's cars or homes, and indifferent to the impact that their noisy or anti-social behaviour has on fellow residents whether their housing is new or old.

THE POOR IN A TRAP

Very soon after the passage of the Homeless Persons and Race Relations legislation in the 1970s a still more significant change came, not to change the ordering of demand, but to curtail supply. The Conservative government further restricted the building of new social housing almost immediately after it was elected in 1979. Between 1979 and 1997 housing declined from being 6.26 per cent of annual public spending to 1.3 per cent according to Treasury figures.[34] In 1980, £5.6 billion was spent on housing. By 1996 it had fallen to £4.8 billion. In the same period public spending had risen from £92.2 billion to £268.8 billion. In 1980 there were 74,835 completions of new housing by local authorities. By 1995 this had dropped right away to 817. This was to some extent offset by the growth in completions by housing associations – 19,299 in 1980 and 31,068 by 1995.[35] Nonetheless, the overall falling away was drastic. On top of all this, 1.5 million homes were lost to the public sector through the exercise of the right to buy, a sale that produced receipts to local authorities of £25 billion – more than from any other single privatisation, but not ones which the councils to which the receipts accrued were allowed unfettered access, because of the prohibition of the government on the spending of those monies.

Nor was it just the cities that felt the strain of short supply. The Rural Development Commission's *Lifestyles* report found that in all the 12 rural areas they surveyed very high proportions of respondents – as high as 90 per cent in Yorkshire and more than 60 per cent in all other areas except one – thought local people were experiencing difficulties in getting the sort of accommodation they wanted. Young people in particular were experiencing the greatest difficulties, and the limited availability of rented homes was raised in all areas.[36] In 1997 the Housing Corporation had a target of 1,500 approvals of new homes in rural areas.[37] It seems unlikely to be enough.

The Homeless Persons Act and the decline in building new social housing combined to ensure that the proportion of lettings going to homeless people has increased substantially. Between 1990 and 1996 the proportion of new lettings by housing associations to people who had been homeless increased by 72 per cent.[38] There have been significant regional variations as well, London having to deal with a large share of such households, about 30 per cent on average,[39] causing even greater pressure on demand for social housing in the capital.

The other outcome of this great demand but short supply is the growing proportion of people in social housing either unemployed or living on welfare benefits, because it is the poorest whose need is of the highest priority. In 1981, 43 per cent of council tenants were in full-time employment and 42 per cent of housing association tenants. By 1988 this had declined to 26 per cent and 25 per cent respectively. By 1994/95 it had declined yet further to 21 per cent of council tenants and 21 per cent of housing association tenants. The average incomes of council tenants fell from three quarters of the national average in 1980 to less than half (48 per cent) by 1990. By 1994 it had fallen to a third of national income. Half of new tenants have a household income of less than £75 per week.[40] The proximity of large enclaves of social housing to erstwhile, enormous manufacturing employers – shipbuilders, steelworks, car factories, coalmines – meant that the carnage that was wrought in the manufacturing sector during the 1980s in which more than 1.8 million jobs were casualties, turned viable, multi-generational communities into concentrations of what some are describing as the underclass – one of the prompts for the Government in establishing a Social Exclusion Unit in 1997 led by the Prime Minister. Those that can, leave; those that remain, cannot. This was not just due to increasing numbers of unemployed people but also to larger numbers of older people and single parents. Forty-five per cent of council tenants were pensioners by 1990. Amongst council tenants, of all households with children under 16, 39 per cent were lone parents. Forty-four per cent of housing associations' households with children under 16 were lone parents. For new tenants the disparity between social housing and other tenures is most marked. Fifty-six per cent of new council tenants and 53 per cent of new housing association tenants with children under 16 are lone parents. By comparison the figure for all tenures is 16 per cent.[41] Social housing tenants are now among the poorest of the poor, many segregated in veritable ghettos of poverty. And there are other deprivations faced by these tenants: secondary schools serving the twenty estates that Anne Power revisited performed far worse than the national average. Less than half got five or more GCSE passes at A to C level. Four times the number of children from estate-linked schools got no GCSEs at all compared with the local authorities in the study as a whole. One in six pupils on estate-linked schools were absent from school registration for at least one half-day session in a term. Nationally the figure is one in eleven.[42]

Poverty which was already growing more concentrated in social housing has turned into a trap because of a very rapid rise in social housing rents. Housing association "fair rents" have risen from £12.52 in 1980 to £43.88 in 1995. Assured rents were £24.50 per week on their introduction in 1989. By 1995 they had risen to £48.29. Average rent on new housing association homes in the first three months of 1997 was £59.37. Council rents have rocketed too. The average council rent was £7.70 in 1980 and by 1995 had risen to £38.31. Even though the rents are paid in many cases by housing benefit, the poverty trap has significantly deepened. Between 64 per cent and 70 per cent of new housing association rents are not "affordable", housing costs being more than 25 per cent of household income.[43] A fairly well-paid job is needed to escape. According to Frank Field, two thirds of job openings offer pay of less than £75 a week.[44] The poverty trap has sides as high as a canyon. In 1997 the Government announced that they were asking the Housing Corporation to monitor rents to bring them down by four per cent. This is welcome, of course, but will only ameliorate not remove what has happened.

A CRISIS OF CRIME

Research showing that England and Wales have the highest levels of crime in the industrialised world has served to heighten the sense of crisis.[45] And it is not just burglary and theft. Crimes against the person, vandalism and disturbance are all a top political priority. These concerns loom much larger in social housing.

> Criminologists Tony Bottoms and Paul Wiles have observed that "late modern society" is characterised by community fragmentation, increased personal insecurity, social isolation and a decline in community cohesion and the stability of the family. They note how our cities are in danger of dividing into two types of areas. On the one hand, there are the shopping malls, office complexes and up-market estates which are privately owned, safe, well-policed and able to exclude those who are considered undesirable. On the other, there are social housing estates and public spaces which have minimum levels of policing and low levels of social control, which are termed the "badlands".[46]

There are numerous examples. One is the Aylsebury estate in South London. It has gained a certain notoriety because it is one of the largest social housing estates in Europe with 12,000 residents and was the venue for Tony Blair's first speech after becoming Prime Minister. It is owned and managed by the London Borough of Southwark. Lorraine Lauder, Chair of Taplow Neighbourhood Forum, revealed an alarming and striking statistic in *The Guardian*, "Crime has improved, but in the last couple of years all 29 sheltered housing units (for older people) have been robbed by kids as young as 12." Nonetheless she feels it is "a strong, tightly-knit community."[47]

Reducing the number of poor and homeless people being housed in any one place has been proposed as a solution in the belief that that will also reduce the amount of anti-social conduct. The question of where the unfortunate so excluded might go has not been so thoroughly addressed. Apart from not housing the anti-social in the first place the clamour has also grown to make it easier for social landlords to evict tenants who are themselves vandals, or violent, or extremely noisy, or whose family or friends are any or all of the above. The Housing Act 1996 is a response to these concerns and should make it easier to evict disruptive or criminal tenants. New grounds for possession were introduced dealing both with anti-social behaviour and criminal conduct. These new grounds make it easier for courts to act on the evidence of housing managers or police officers. The period of notice for serious nuisance can also now be very short; the same day if necessary. Injunctions can also now have the power of arrest attached. Breaching the injunction could bring a criminal penalty for contempt of court and the penalty could be a good deal heavier than penalties attached to the original anti-social behaviour or criminal conduct. Nonetheless, the belief that housing managers can produce good behaviour by the deterrent impact of threatening eviction is a fallacy which, if clung to, will prove expensive in the suffering of tenants as well as in management time.

Reducing anti-social behaviour takes more than just excluding those thought likely to become anti-social and throwing out those who in fact become so.

> If we want to prevent crime in those areas where high standards do not prevail, we must intervene in the process which leads to a crime being committed. We must focus on the crime-prone situation and make the crime more difficult to commit. Similarly, if we want to reduce criminality, we must intervene in the circumstances that prevent some young people learning to behave socially, failing to respect others and growing up to believe that they have no stake in society.[48]

But who must intervene? Landlords are not sure it is their job; how much could they afford to do to the buildings and the environment? Would it have any impact anyway? Certainly in North Kensington improvements were made to the strength of doors, particularly to basement flats, lighting and other security measures. These improvements were offered to homeowners as well as social housing tenants. The police can have only a limited effect on the physical improvements that might prevent crime in the home or on the street. The schools certainly have a role. Local authorities too. But once more it seems to many, including the writers we have already quoted, that the undermining of the family, the neighbourhood and the community is at the heart of the matter; the heart of both the problem and the solution.

*　　　　*　　　　*

In this chapter we have been reviewing the history of housing policy and its relationship to community and the manifestations of mutual aid which are intrinsic to community. The history has taken us back to the 1950s, and the communities we have lost since then. Despite many achievements, notably the building of a large number of new homes, and increasing space standards and amenities, housing policy over this whole period has not been by any means part of a seamless web. Policy has leaned one way and then another, with one common thread being that social housing allocations have been said to be governed by "need". But the shifts and turns in interpretation of need have produced a compromise. Few people, however well-intentioned, have the assurance that what they are doing currently is absolutely right, as our survey showed. It is time for a change; it is time for a new start and in the next chapter we suggest some of the steps which could be taken.

Encouragement of Informal Mutual Aid

So much for where we are. How to get from where we are to where we want to be? To make this crucial journey we need pointers to show the way ahead. Some of these are already implicit and now have to be made explicit. This we do under three main headings. The first is about the manner in which new housing and vacancies in existing housing are allocated. The second is about the additional encouragement to mutuality which could be given by a new Mutual Aid Compact which people would be asked to sign at the same time as they enter into new social housing tenancy agreements, mutuality and morality being almost synonymous with each other. The third is a new organisation with the encouragement of mutuality as its specific purpose – the Mutual Aid Housing Advisory Centre.

Despite all the consequences of rationing social housing that we discussed in the last chapter there can be no question of pushing aside housing need and substituting social need – the bonds and ties of community and family – instead. Local authorities have the duty to register the people in their districts who want new social housing and to line them up in order of their *housing need*, even while they have been denied the ability to expand the capacity to meet the housing need themselves. This duty could not easily be performed on their own by housing associations who are not accountable to an electorate and do not cover the whole area of a local authority. So waiting lists, or registers as they are starting to be known, have by and large continued to be administered by local authorities who nominate most of the housing associations' tenants, reflecting the fact that most new social housing was by the late 1980s being provided by housing associations not councils.

There it is and there is no case for dismantling the present system notwithstanding our many criticisms of how it has worked in practice. It is undeniably equitable. It is, for instance, obviously fair that someone with nowhere at all to live should have the highest priority and that a family which is overcrowded in its present accommodation – say with six children in a two-bedroom property – should be rehoused before a family with two children in a one-bedroom property; or a family with a home with an outside toilet and no hot water take precedence over one already with an inside toilet and a hot water supply. Following this line of moral justification, councils with a shortage of housing and a need for waiting lists therefore have more or less elaborate methods of scoring relative needs and calibrating them to compare one applicant with another. A person or family with more points is preferred to one with less whenever a vacancy occurs. A points system can cover the following kinds of needs, to give an example from one local authority.

Extra bedroom required	40 points
No bathroom	20 points
Opposite sexes sharing a bedroom (other than partners)	25 points
Medical needs	200 points
Moving to smaller accommodation	50 points per room saved.

MUTUALITY POINTS

Local authorities are already required by Section 167 of the Housing Act 1996 to give "reasonable preference" to households with a particular need for accommodation on medical or welfare grounds. The "welfare grounds" can be quantified in the same way as housing grounds, comprising different social needs. People may need care of one kind or another from outside their own homes, and that is their social need. The Housing Corporation says in its draft Performance Standards for Registered Social Landlords, "RSLs should normally let their homes to people in greatest housing need. Their lettings policies and practices should be fair, accountable and make the best use of available stock; and they should aim to let tenancies which are sustainable in the long term and contribute to stable communities." It is recognised elsewhere in the same document that in some circumstances meeting "greatest housing need" may run counter to "stable communities" and we have already noted in Chapter 3 some occasions when other priorities have been drawn alongside, or even superceded, meeting the greatest housing need. The Corporation therefore suggests action that housing associations (or registered social landlords as they may be called in the future) can take: "allocations do not have to be made according to highest need…if steps are needed to prevent or reverse social conditions in an area threatening the housing rights of most residents or the value of the stock. If these circumstances can be demonstrated to exist, an RSL may adopt a 'local lettings policy'."

We have an alternative proposal which we believe would be more effective in building sustainable communities and need not be confined to areas of severe social problems. It would not run counter to meeting housing need and so could be applied across the board, not just in demonstrably exceptional circumstances. We are not proposing setting housing need aside but awarding points for social needs as well. The difference in our proposal is that ordinary points attach to the person who is needing housing while the social need points attach to the person who has the social need *or can be transferred to the person who will satisfy the need*. The actual number of points for people in different circumstances would, as at present, be determined by the local authority's housing committee working within the statutory framework.

We can show what we mean by presenting a different kind of points rating which we call mutuality points because they become realisable only when someone else is able by mutual agreement to meet the needs in question. Examples are as follows:

Old person over 70, or younger disabled
    person, who cannot look after himself
    or herself without outside assistance
    (points awarded by the medical adviser
    or the care manager from social or
    health services who is responsible
    for community care assessments)   +100 points
Person of any age, and with any disability,
    who is generally independent, but needs
    some outside assistance with daily

living (points awarded by social services)	+50 points
Single parents (or two parents) who are not able fully to look after their children, whether due to work or other reason without outside assistance for daily living (points awarded by health or social services)	+50 points
Separated parents with shared responsibilities for bringing up children	+50 points

TRANSFERABLE POINTS FOR SOCIAL NEEDS

The whole purpose of the new arrangement would be to bring the homes of people who need each other closer together; the points awarded, say, to an old person would be usable either by the old person in need of care or by the carer who would provide it. An old person would be able to use his or her (or both their) mutuality points when putting in an application to live near, say, a daughter; and a daughter would benefit from the same number of points, assessed by reference to the old persons' needs, if she applied to live near them. The points would, if necessary, be transferable from the older to the younger person since the object of the exercise would be achieved either by the younger moving nearer the older or vice versa.

Sometimes the only way to get closer together would be for the pair to move together to a new settlement or into existing housing. How would the points be calculated and assigned then? If the old person moved near the daughter, the old person would have his or her own social need points to constitute the claim to a measure of priority. If the daughter moved near the old person, the daughter would be credited with the old person's mutuality points. They would each have the same number of points even though they could only be activated by moving together. But if they both had to move to come together they would each carry their points with them. If they did not, not only would they be at a disadvantage compared to the situation where only one of them had to move, but the purpose of the whole arrangement would be lost. It would be futile for, say, an elderly widow to be rehoused on a new estate by using her mutuality points unless her daughter could also move there to satisfy those needs. To understand how the new system would work in practice, it is worth pointing out some of its main features.

"Near" could be defined in different ways. Within a ten minute journey would be reasonable enough. All that we have said would, of course, be turned the opposite way around when an older person or couple was going to look after the children of parents who needed support. The older person would borrow the points of the younger.

Mutuality points for social needs would be added to any points attributed for housing needs. A daughter whose accommodation was overcrowded could get 65 points for that. If she wanted to be near her mother who was not disabled but needing some assistance and so got 50 points for that, she would have a total points rating of 115.

The beneficiaries on both sides would usually be relatives and even then the persons in need of care would have to agree that they wanted the particular caring relative to be near them. Ordinarily, it would be a matter for relatives. But if a friend or neighbour were prepared to offer care and were accepted as such by the person to be cared for, that person should be able to "borrow" the mutuality points in the same way as a relative.

The main objective – carers living near to each other so that people in need would be looked after without being a cost to the state over many years – could be more easily achieved where the housing was on a new estate or in a new cluster (though we may recognise that the more usual case is that it is existing housing that is being let). There would however be occasions when a number of vacancies would appear in the same place at the same time. Cared and carers could move near to each other simultaneously because they moved together. Indeed, a proportion of the new dwellings could be given over to extended families. This would be in accord with the practice of local authorities and housing associations which decide on the percentage of empty properties which will over a year be offered to a particular target group like 30 per cent for the homeless, eight per cent for people suffering harassment, six per cent for people in urgent need on health grounds and so forth. It could be laid down as part of a lettings plan that, say, 30 per cent of new properties in a new scheme could be kept for people in the social needs category. That would also help in seeing that three generational mutual aid was well represented in the new settlement and this would influence the tone of other relationships in the place.

It would not be so simple to achieve this object where vacancies were generated in the ordinary stock of houses when a tenant moved or died. When either the cared for or the carer was living near the vacant dwelling a check could be made to see if either of them on the register had enough points on all grounds to be offered the tenancy. But if both members of a family had to move to be near each other, it is unlikely that two properties suitable for the size of their families would become vacant at the same time. It would not make sense to keep one property empty for many weeks in the hope that another one would soon come along that would constitute the right match. Some leeway could be given to the housing managers to keep a property void for a little longer than usual if there was any reason to think that another suitable place would be vacated soon. But voids on any scale are clearly not to be encouraged for too long.

There would be a great advantage in making the scheme as nationwide as possible. Very many young mothers (as we have seen) live within five miles of their mothers. Though not necessarily near enough to each other for daily care to be possible, there is a reasonable chance of members of extended families living within the area of the same local authority. But many families are also dispersed: everywhere, older people have been left behind by their adult children who have moved elsewhere for advancement in their jobs, for the quality of their housing, or to places where schools are better for their children. If the older people could transfer their points to the district where their child or children now live – once again as long as the adult child in question was willing, supply and demand permitting – there could be a considerable ingathering of families all over the country at a time when their older members were having to cope with increasing frailty. All this could be an additional element in the existing national mobility scheme (HOMES).

NOT JUST FAMILIES

Despite the durability of the three generational extended family, social changes have meant that more people live on their own and many women either opt not to have children at all, or have them much later. The social movements of the 1970s such as feminism and gay liberation and the more recent environmental movement have led to many alternative lifestyles which brought people together in relationships of care and support even when they were not related by kin. These arrangements too need to be validated and encouraged, for they too are ties of mutuality which, for some single people, are on a par with their relationships within their family.

We have seen a small amount of this during the tragedy of AIDS where gay men found themselves caring for their dying fellows at a much younger age than was commonly the case. Many people moved nearer to each other to give this care, both partners and friends. Complicated networks and rotas were put in place which could only work on the basis that people lived near one another. Some local authorities even gave some priority for social housing not just to the person with AIDS, but also to their carers.

A STATUTORY BASIS FOR MUTUALITY POINTS AND SOCIAL NEEDS

We do not think that new legislation is needed for the establishment of a system of transferable mutuality points for social needs. Indeed the current Department of the Environment Code of Guidance on the Housing Act 1996 talks at paragraph 5.6 of ensuring a "viable social mix". The problem may be, given the importance that we attach to making the scheme national, that some local authorities might not recognise social needs and mutuality points. To forestall that possibility we would recommend that, in due course, transferable priority for social needs be built into the official guidance.

The question of rationing and of new entitlements for acceptance in the queue is only one aspect of an even more important subject: the size of the housing programme and its character. If only certain sizes and types of houses are going to be in demand from people who want to live closer together, then the supply of that type of house is going to be the limiting factor. The obvious example is of relatively small houses for elderly couples and older widowed people on their own – particularly women who ordinarily live so much longer than men. They need houses which are fine for them when they are hearty members of the Third Age enjoying life to the full, including their grandparenthood; and are also fine – easy to maintain, arranged for people who are getting frail – for the same people when they grow still older.

Housing associations and local authorities are finding some sheltered housing in a block solely for old people harder to let. These blocks were often designed to be under the care of a warden who was not a relative of any of the tenants or owners. Impersonality was one of its distinguishing marks. A new sort of sheltered housing is needed (that is with space for grandchildren to stay) and sheltered housing (for when the time of fading independence comes) should be in "single spies, not battalions", and scattered near wherever young married people are. There should then be a better chance of achieving the new housing ideal of mutual aid matches. The right kind of housing could be as attractive for private builders to provide as for local authorities and housing associations.

POTENTIAL OBJECTIONS

But are we not just adding yet more obligations to the already over-extended social housing system? Will not the effect be to give yet more people a claim to social housing when we cannot even meet the current needs? And would not the arrangements proposed here put black and minority ethnic people at a disadvantage? These are some of the potential objections, and they are real ones. But there are adequate responses. Firstly, we accept that there are parts of the country where there is a need for more social housing and, without that, it will be difficult to meet the housing needs that already exist, never mind meeting the new obligations that we are proposing to house those with social needs. We fervently hope that the availability of capital receipts and capital funds to the Housing Corporation will mean some of this shortfall can be met.

There is not a shortage of social housing everywhere. We have already discussed hard-to-let social housing in Chapter 3. Nor is it only older, run-down estate-based housing that is sometimes not much in demand. A recent study made the somewhat alarming discovery that up to one third of newly refurbished units of social housing in parts of the north of England were hard to let on first letting.[1] So there are currently places where giving priority to social needs could be easily achieved because the housing is available. Dealing with low demand and meeting social needs would be a most felicitous combination for many social housing landlords.

"Carefully organised lettings and management control are not the same as discrimination, although this has been suggested by some. Discrimination usually works in much more subtle and pervasive ways."[2] The assertion that it was the sons and daughters policy which led to discrimination in social housing was always contentious and Anne Power, quoted above, is arguing that a local phenomenon of systematic discrimination was ascribed a national cause and national consequences. The true causes of the disadvantage faced by black and minority ethnic people in getting social housing was, and is, in part the consequence of the prejudices of allocators, as well as, in some places, systematic forms of indirect discrimination. But a far more widespread and damaging phenomenon is the impact of higher levels of poverty and unemployment on the ability of black and ethnic minority people to assert and achieve their own housing aspirations. They have that in common with all those who are poor and unemployed. Colour and ethnicity is not the only consideration.

Longer established black and minority ethnic communities are in a wholly different position to new arrivals when it comes to the search for good housing. Much of the indirect discrimination we described in Chapter 3 – the treatment of separated families, the residential qualification, sons and daughters policies – put people at a disadvantage because they were relative newcomers. The black communities originating from the ex-colonies who formed the great wave of post-war migration are now in their second, third and the beginning of the fourth generation. There is little reason to suppose that an allocation system which took into account social needs and the bonds with families and friends that people have established to meet those social needs would put these groups at a disadvantage, especially as many of them too now have grown-up sons and daughters whom they would like to live nearby. Restrictions on immigration have meant that most of those people still arriving in Britain with a need for social housing are refugees and asylum seekers. They are very often homeless and, so long as priority is given to homeless people, they should not suffer a disadvantage. Refugees are also the very people who need the support of their community.

Many organisations are alarmed by the treatment of refugees and asylum seekers in search of housing. Local authorities are in many cases statutorily prevented from offering social housing. Social services departments, on the other hand, are obliged to help under the National Assistance Act 1948. Because they cannot use local social housing they have been forced to house refugees many miles from their chosen place of settlement. In conducting interviews for a research project into black and minority ethnic housing needs in London for the Housing Corporation one of us has heard of Somali refugees, often single parents with families of small children or adults disabled in war, who have arrived in London and then been housed in Eastbourne and Liverpool. And it is not the first time it has happened. Similar policies of dispersal, though for different reasons, were followed in the early 1980s when the so-called "boat people" arrived from Vietnam. Proximity to social support is arguably more important after the traumas of fear, expulsion and loss of homeland than in any other circumstances. Suggesting that seeking to meet social needs by ensuring proximity to friends, relatives and carers would put refugees at a disadvantage seems, in this light, a perverse conclusion.

The upsurge of skills and talents, coupled with the support of the Housing Corporation, that has given rise to such a thriving group of black housing associations across the country is also evidence of the wish on the part of black communities to organise themselves in a way that simultaneously maximises the involvement and self-help of the community while at the same time accessing public funds to do those things, such as building social housing, that cannot be achieved solely through the sterling efforts of volunteers and social entrepreneurs. Black associations are a good example, to our mind, of a social policy initiative which has brought the resources of the state into harness with the gifts and unpaid commitments of those who knew that something needed to be done and had a good idea what it was.[3] This is an example of the combination of formal and informal mutual aid that is at the heart of this book's proposals.

It will, we hope, be possible by the means we have described to encourage stability of residence and proximity of support from family or others through the system for allocating social housing, but yet more could be done to enable community building in the arrangements that are made for the management of the housing. It is to that we turn next.

NEGATIVES AND POSITIVES IN THE TENANCY AGREEMENT

Now that we come to our second subject, the standard form of tenancy agreement in social housing is not sufficient for the building of community. Like any other contract, agreements are nearly all about the obligation of the one party to another: on the one hand the landlord's obligations for repairs, maintenance, caretaking, cleaning and gardening. The tenant, as the other party, has obligations to pay rent and service charges and grant access to the landlord to do repairs. The agreement is between two parties, and to this there is only one exception, but one which we can build on.

The exception is about what tenants (and their children and visitors) are not supposed to do to their neighbours – not to harass them or to cause a nuisance to them. If the offence is persistent and formal warnings are brushed off the landlord can go to the courts who may injunct the tenant against the behaviour which has so upset the neighbours. If all else fails, the courts can allow the landlord to evict the tenant. Legal remedies there must be, including eviction. The law has been strengthened as a result of campaigning by deeply frustrated tenants and housing managers. The last resort of the landlord taking possession of the tenant's home must remain. Furthermore, people evicted because of the nuisance they have caused may be judged "intentionally homeless". Housing departments then have no further obligation to house them, whether or not they have children who may be guiltless. Moves towards "probationary" or "introductory" tenancies for new tenants have reinforced the requirement of good behaviour. People may lose their home if they do not behave in line with the requirements of the tenancy agreement and, because they are new tenants and therefore in a sense "on trial", breaches may lose them their home in short order. Anti-social tenants are not the only ones liable for penalty; even perfectly well-behaved tenants with badly behaved children or unruly visitors are for it. Courts have certainly been willing to evict tenants for the behaviour of their children. The Court of Appeal seems to have been sending out a strong message to county courts: evict the anti-social.[4] The Englishman's home may be his castle, but he now has to be very careful that he does not allow his bowmen to upset their counterparts at the ready in the castle next door.

So it is not quite right to say there are only two parties to the agreement – the landlord, the tenant and (this is the rub) the neighbours make it three. But all that is laid down about behaviour towards neighbours is negative. The tenant and the others for whom he or she is pronounced responsible are not to do this, and not to do that. The little society is filled with negatives. There is no call for anything positive. This distinction is similar to the famous one made by Isaiah Berlin between the two sorts of freedom, "freedom from" (the negative, coercion, infringement of one's rights etc) and "freedom for" (the positive, the realm of human possibility, everything a person can become).[5] The prohibition of anti-social behaviour is for the benefit of neighbours. But there is a strong case for going one further than that and encouraging some positive support for them where they need it, and some positive support the other way round for yourself when you need it. The obligation would be mutual, and could take the form of a Mutual Aid Compact which we will describe below.

ANALOGY OF HOME-SCHOOL CONTRACTS

In proposing the Mutual Aid Compact we have by way of analogy had in mind the home-school contracts which have become part of the common practice of schools. Hitherto a parent's only obligation was to ensure their child attended school everyday on time, or if not, that the school was informed. Failure to ensure the child's attendance brings forth letters from the school and, if they produce no result, the matter is referred to the education authority who would, in extreme circumstances, take legal action against the parent. The parent has no legal obligation to the school. Their legal obligation is to demonstrate to the education authority either that they are ensuring their child's attendance at school or, in rare circumstances, educating them at home to a standard that satisfies the education authority.

In recent times the importance of a more active parental involvement, both in the child's education and the running of the school, has been recognised and encouraged by political parties and educationalists. Home-school contracts have become the way in which the mutual obligations of all three parties – parent, child and school – are made explicit. David Blunkett, the Secretary of State for Education and Employment, has stressed the importance of these contracts in launching his 1997 White Paper, *Excellence in Schools*. The school's relationship is not just with the child, but with the parents too.

> Parents are a child's first teacher. We want to build on this sound beginning of the family learning together by giving the parents the power to improve the education of their children for the rest of their school careers...But with power comes responsibility, so there will be home-school contracts setting out duties and responsibilities of home and school explaining clearly what is expected of both parents and teachers in terms of homework, discipline and attendance.[6]

The school, for their part, agrees to ensure that the child is well taught and develops a sense of responsibility and so forth as has always been their obligation. In return the parent (to quote from a particular agreement for a son) signs an undertaking to:
- see that he comes to school regularly, on time and with all the equipment he needs;

- send a note to the school explaining any absence;
- let the school know about any problems which might affect his work or behaviour;
- support him with reading and other home learning activities;
- check and sign his diary each week;
- encourage him to join the after-school clubs which interest him;
- attend parents' evenings and discussions about his progress;
- support school policies and rules, and the code of conduct on behaviour.

The 1997 White Paper makes it clear that the Government intends to make such contracts a "requirement" for all schools. They recognise that "such agreements will not be legally binding, but they will be powerful statements of intent...They will be important in helping engage parents in raising pupils' achievements and in action to combat truancy, bullying and unacceptable behaviour."[7] So they will be called contracts but they will not be enforcable in a legal sense. There are no penalties for failure to comply; no damages to be paid, nor any suggestion that a child will be denied his or her place at school because of parental shortcoming. The contract is not there to coerce parents into compliance on pain of a fearful or expensive deterrent, but to set clear and explicit standards, create expectations of everyone and diffuse good practice from those who will readily comply to whose who will not. The diffusion will not be by force, but by the power of persuasion and example. And our Mutual Aid Compact for social housing would have the very same goals in mind and be effective in the same way for the same reasons, as we will now go on to describe.

THE MUTUAL AID COMPACT

On the basis of the above analogy we want to propose that new tenants (either in new housing or in the existing housing stock) would be asked to sign a Mutual Aid Compact. This would not be part of the tenancy agreement but in a separate document alongside. The landlord would ask the putative new tenant to sign the Compact before the tenancy was granted. The Compact could take the following form.

THE MUTUAL AID COMPACT

If the community of ....is to be a community based on mutual respect it needs to be:

- a place where there is respect for other's property, where all crime affecting people and property is kept to a minimum;
- a place where there is respect for the environment, ensuring that it is clean and that public areas are kept in good order;
- a place where there is respect for other people's different lifestyles;
- a place where there is respect for open spaces which are safe and pleasant for children to play in and young people and others to meet;
- a place where people already know, or get to know and support one another, especially providing support to those in need of the greatest assistance, such as old or disabled people.

I am willing to make a contribution to the mutual aid needed to create and sustain this community.

I am willing to help my neighbour, or someone else living nearby, with practical support for things they cannot easily do for themselves, by joining a group dedicated to giving this practical support.

I am willing to make the annual mutual aid commitment to this community, identifying what I can offer to the community, and what support I need.

Signed by all adults in the household.............................

AN EXPECTATION OF NEW TENANTS?

We have acknowledged the potential objections to mutuality points. Some people may also object to the Mutual Aid Compact, or rather to the suggestion that all new tenants should be expected to sign it. "Surely," one argument might run, "it is hard enough already for people in need to get social housing. Signing the Compact is yet another obstacle at a most vulnerable time in people's lives – when they have been homeless or in housing need. What happens if a would be tenant refuses to sign?" Our intention is not to make it harder for people to get housed, but to establish clearly when people move in the expectation in their minds that living in a community which is strong, safe and supportive, requires a contribution from them to that community. In the same way, a parent who sends their child to school is being expected to recognise the contribution they must make to the successful education of their child. If new tenants are worried about what will happen to them if they do not, or cannot, make a contribution of mutual aid, they can be reassured that they do not have to sign the Compact and that it is not legally enforceable as we will explain below, so they are not at risk of being denied an offer or of losing their homes as they would be if they persistently breached any of the requirements of the tenancy agreement.

If the Mutual Aid Compact is offered as an agreement alongside all new local authority and other social landlords' tenancy agreements, over time the numbers of new residents who have signed will increase. Mutual aid could become more and more common and a neighbourly custom created where it did not exist. Where it did, it would be reinforced. Where a new estate was built or substantially refurbished, or demolished and rebuilt, all the tenants moving in could be asked to sign. The far larger number of tenants who move in when there is a vacancy in existing stock would also be asked to sign the Mutual Aid Compact. Existing tenants also could be asked to sign the Compact.

If some of the people identified by local authorities as being in need of housing feel that their existing commitments or their own needs create circumstances in which they would find it difficult to fulfil the mutual aid requirement, the prospective landlord would look on these limitations benignly. It is not our intention that the Mutual Aid Compact is a "rigid fetter" on how authorities exercise their discretion in allocating tenancies. People who for reasons of their own needs and commitments cannot fulfill the requirement should not be denied social housing if they need it; as we said earlier, the principle of allocating social housing according to need is right and equitable, with the proviso we have stated: that social needs as well as housing needs should be taken into account.

PERSUASION OR ENFORCEMENT

We are not proposing that a tenant who fails to demonstrate pro-social behaviour, in other words who ignores the Mutual Aid Compact, should even in an extreme case be evicted, just as a child will not be turned away from school because their parents have not fulfilled the requirements of the home-school contract. We think that even at the extreme it would be going too far. Mutual aid, to be acceptable, cannot be given in a grudging spirit, which it well might be, if the aid was forthcoming only because behind it lay the threat of coercion. Tenants can be asked to sign the new Compact; they cannot be required to act on it on pain of penalty, which is the reason the Compact is not being proposed as part of the tenancy agreement, all the clauses of which are enforceable. People cannot be compelled to be kind to one another. If they could, governments would have lost many of their roles long ago. To deserve the name, mutual aid has to be willingly given and willingly received, without coercion.

We have said that the Mutual Aid Compact would not be enforceable in law. Does this mean it would be pointless? Not at all. It would still have a considerable point to it. Even without ultimate sanction it would be the prompter for a new expectation: that those who benefit from social housing and the element of subsidy for it which comes from taxpayers in general should reciprocate by being willing to offer help to neighbours and others who need it. The object is to build up a new body of custom and practice, amongst existing and new tenants, which will not have the deterrent of possible eviction behind it but the persuasive force of custom.

Good, as well as bad, behaviour can be diffused. The best known demonstration of this is the analysis by Bruce Ryan and Neal Gross of the spread of hybrid seed corn in Greene County, Iowa. Introduced in 1928, the new seed corn was superior in every respect, but it was not adopted immediately by wary farmers. Only a handful of 259 farmers had adopted it by 1932 and 1933. In 1934 16 took the plunge. In 1935 21 followed, then 36, then 61, then 46, then 36, 14 and 3. By 1941 all but two of 259 had started using the new seed corn. The pattern, which if charted on a graph would be a bell curve, is of innovators, followed by early adopters, then the early majority, followed by the late majority, and the laggards. The method of diffusion was almost entirely through word of mouth. In our proposal, there could be diffusion of mutual aid beyond social housing rather more quickly than the spread of the new seed corn. We have shown in our survey reported in Chapter 2 how in recent times there has been a diffusion of housing plus activities amongst housing associations. Projects for young people and children, local employment initiatives and so on have been taken up by the few, followed by the many and finally taken up by the cautious and the reluctant.

The chances of the Mutual Aid Compact creating a new custom would be less if we were seeking something entirely new. We are not. Informal mutual aid, in and out of families, is nothing new, as we have already seen in Chapter 3. There is already plenty of it. What we are seeking is to add to it, achieved not through the law but by persuasion. This should never be undervalued as a means of support for custom and a means of bringing about new custom. If possession is nine points of the law, persuasion is nine points of custom. In this respect there is something to learn from Sir Thomas More's attitude to laws in his *Utopia*.

> They have very few laws, because, with their social system, very few laws are required. Indeed, one of their great complaints against other countries is that, although they've already got books of law and interpretations of laws, they never seem to have enough. For, according to the Utopians, it's quite unjust for anyone to be bound by a legal code which is too long for an ordinary person to read right through, or too difficult for him to understand. What's more, they have no barristers to be over-ingenious about individual cases and points of law. They think it better for each man to plead his own cause, and tell the judge the same story as he'd otherwise tell his lawyer. Under such conditions, the point at issue is less likely to be obscured, and it's easier to get at the truth – for, if nobody's telling the sort of lies that one learns from lawyers, the judge can apply all his shrewdness to weighing the facts of the case, and protecting simple-minded characters against the unscrupulous attacks of clever ones.[8]

IMPLEMENTING THE MUTUAL AID COMPACT

To persuade needs to be someone's responsibility if mutual aid is to become more common. If something of the sort were not being done already, the diffusion would take longer. But it is being done already, although not on nearly as large a scale as it could be.

Many local authorities and housing associations already employ housing support workers (going under different names). They may be called in to support a vulnerable tenant whose behaviour is felt by others to be anti-social. The flat may be in disrepair or the rent not being regularly paid. Perhaps the tenant has moved in from a hostel or temporary accommodation needing some assistance with resettlement. This may be the tenant's first experience of independent living after a long time of institutionalisation. The role of the housing support worker is to ensure that a vulnerable tenant receives the support they need so they can enjoy the comfort of home at peace with their neighbours and fulfilling the requirements of the tenancy agreement. Bringing in volunteers, local church people and voluntary organisations to give care and support alongside formal support is often a means of achieving this.

Our suggestion is that the social landlord should be much more pro-active than is often the case, not just in dealing with anti-social behaviour but encouraging practical co-operation. A new function needs to be recognised, that of co-ordinating mutual aid, and it could be performed by a person being appointed for specifically that purpose or by adding to the functions of one or more members of a housing support team. It is worth saying a word about the functions envisaged for those with the new role.

The first function would be to seek outside aid for any tenant who is in social need and not yet being supported. It could mean calling in a paid social worker from the social services department who can assess the needs of the tenant and provide access to other paid people in the form of a care package. Or it might be a home help, a district nurse or a volunteer from Age Concern or another voluntary body who would be more appropriate.

The second function, performed once a year, would be to see all the new tenants who have signed the Mutual Aid Compact and discuss with them what they might be prepared to do for other tenants and their families, if, indeed, they are not already helping out in one way or another, as many of them would be. They would not, we think, be introduced to another person needing help. The co-ordinator would not be able to be sure about the genuineness of someone who showed willingness, even eagerness to be the provider of aid. There would be too much risk attached to introducing him or her alone into the privacy of someone else's home.

For such reasons it should be the norm that everyone not ruled out by reason of the mutual aid already being given would be put in touch with a church, tenants' association or other voluntary body which would find out as much as they ordinarily did about anyone who was ready to join their ranks. The advantage to the voluntary bodies would be that they could gain additional members and new volunteers. All around the country there are volunteer centres and volunteer co-ordinators that would very much appreciate the extra help. Even some housing associations now have volunteer co-ordinators, drawing in people, not always their own tenants, to help the organisation or to help each other. We are a long way from more help being available than is needed.

Levels of volunteering are increasing in our society and research at Manchester University has noted how contracting out of social services has increased the role and contribution of volunteers. Cynically, one might imagine that this was motivated by a wish solely to save money. But reality is always more complex and paradoxical than cynics allow. In fact the role of volunteers is becoming more skilled and formalised. Chief officers of voluntary organisations anticipate that the long-term impact will be to enhance the status and value of volunteers. Many existing volunteers felt increased satisfaction, even if "the balance between the costs and benefits of volunteering may be precarious".9

The third function would be to work with tenants to help to set up new voluntary bodies and associations of different kinds where there were people who wanted to join them and be active in them. We envisage a situation where more and more local services could be provided through mutual aid. We have talked about the care of older and disabled people. We have talked also about the care of children. But we would hope to go further. Local authorities and housing associations could use the mutual aid commitments of local people to assist with improving the environment. We were told how much, on one estate, the sight of local residents themselves doing the landscaping of the estate that they had taken over from the council built their confidence and impressed others around who were not involved. We would also want to see tenants encouraged to initiate and organise more formal multilateral mutual aid, such as the formation of credit unions and local exchange trading schemes which were mentioned in Chapter 2.

The benefits of all these mutual aid activities would go far beyond the question of neighbourliness, though that is important enough. The confidence and capacity of people in some of the poorest areas of this country would be built on and expanded. As Perri 6, director of policy and research at the think tank Demos, wrote in *The Guardian* on 3 September 1997,

> Those benefit offices that treat an unemployed person who does voluntary work as not actively seeking or available for work are simply compounding the problem. Not only do many people move from volunteer to paid work, they gain invaluable new contacts. Volunteering is one of the best predictors of moving into the middle class. It's not just the benefits system. The British way of tackling unemployment typically relies on formal labour market institutions, rather than informal networks... A well-known American study a few years ago found that one of the best ways to predict whether an unemployed person would get a job was to check whether they attended church. The reason was nothing to do with the morality or work discipline of practising Christians. Rather, church provides a uniquely valuable place to meet people who can help you find work.

The social benefits of care and support being given by people who live nearby might also be considerable. The loss of the long-standing postman, dinner lady and, most commonly mentioned, the beat bobby has been much mourned. So much so that all political parties regularly promise to "put bobbies back on the beat". Their passing is mourned for more than sentimental reasons. Familiarity with local people outside the family does not always or of necessity breed contempt. A sense of security may also be bred particularly amongst children and old people. Old people are often chided for an unjustified fear of crime. A lack of familiarity with the people working as well as living in the neighbourhood may contribute to this insecurity.

Tenants could do their own maintenance, if they were able, calling on builders or the landlord only for more difficult repairs; or maintenance could be done on a mutual aid basis between neighbours; or maintenance and repairs services could be provided by community businesses established for the purpose, such as Newham Wise which we described in Chapter 2. This would have the subsidiary benefit of generating opportunities for training and the employment of local people, so taking them from welfare to work. Some housing associations are already talking of forming local maintenance companies and Anthony Mayer, the Chief Executive of the Housing Corporation, spoke at a consultation meeting of the London Housing Federation in June 1997 of the need for tenants to gain employment opportunities in housing associations and, we would hope, not just in relation to building and the environment. Local people, having gained some experience of child care or the care of older people could, if they have an aptitude, train to be professional carers as we described in Chapter 2. Local authorities already pay through community care assessment for an enormous amount of home care – £2.4 billion worth in fact.[10] Why should local people, hopefully known and nearby, not gain the skills and rewards of professionalism? That would bring neighbourliness and financial return to a community into a much closer harmony, removing a current economic and geographical dislocation between work for pay and work for mutual aid. If stability of residence is to be encouraged as we discussed in Chapter 3, long-term local jobs will be needed.

There are precedents for some of these local management and maintenance arrangements. Residents' Democracy is the name given to a management model developed for social rented housing in Denmark in the early 1970s. The idea is one of a partnership between landlords and tenants. So instead of all social housing tenants receiving the same services regardless of what an individual or a community wants, the landlord provides services to an agreed service specification which is managed and costed separately for each estate. The tenants have rights which allow them to influence the content and scope of the service provided. The rent is set to reflect these highly local arrangements.[11]

In Britain the Tenants' Guarantee means that the Housing Corporation requires all housing associations they regulate and supervise to deliver the same range of services. Far greater variety in the levels of service offered by housing associations is possible. A real possibility would be created that tenants could contribute through mutual aid and local community businesses and so possibly reduce the rents. There could be no more urgent priority in social housing. Reductions in rents would soon bring down the exploding housing benefit bill. Lower rents would make the climb out of the poverty trap less steep than is currently the case.

This is not such a radical departure as it might sound. The compulsory competitive tendering of housing management that the previous government introduced has been in the minds of many local government officers a bureaucratic, wasteful and fruitless process. However, where the process of competitive tendering has been handled well, the level of service has been very directly related to the cost in terms of current rents and potential rent rises. At its most effective, tenants have had a part in deciding the levels and types of service they want.[12] A strong element of local consultation and involvement in defining local priorities and standards of service is possible. Local authorities in partnership with local people could decide which of the three economic pumps that exist to deliver goods and services in our society – the private sector, the public sector and mutual aid – is best equipped to do what in the management and maintenance of social housing, and indeed many other local services. Once the consultation is complete, standards of service have tended to be specified across the council's whole stock. We would wish to see more local arrangements for specific neighbourhoods, giving tenants the choice and the involvement that might toll the bell for the last vestiges of insensitive and bureaucratic housing management.

There is much to be done by the co-ordinators of mutual aid working for social landlords as we have shown. We would place one further responsibility on them. Tenants need to know what actually has been done by way of mutual aid in the places where they live. So housing associations and local authority housing departments should include in their annual reports an account of what the unsatisfied social needs are and the extent to which social needs have been met by mutual aid and in other ways.

A NATIONAL APPROACH

The Mutual Aid Compact would, we hope, contribute to reinforcing and creating neighbourly customs and, in that way, build the much sought but often elusive spirit of community. It would be a simple, practical means to bring an ideal nearer to a reality, seeking to use a *formal*, if straightforward, method to bring about more *infor-*

mal mutual aid. Some would say that mutual aid can only ever be informal; a willing exchange between family members or friends. There is no place in such arrangements for landlords and involving the law in these arrangements would be inimical to the essence of mutual aid. We have argued that landlords could play a very proactive role in encouraging mutual aid to build sustainable communities. It might indeed assist the landlords themselves to deal with repairs and maintenance, anti-social behaviour and rent arrears and to maintain the value of their stock as we described from the responses to our survey in Chapter 2.

It is clear from what we have seen and written up here that many social landlords are indeed taking on this more proactive, enabling role, though perhaps not always with the specific focus on encouraging reciprocal and multilateral mutual aid that we would like to see. But such activities should not be confined to the enlightened few, or even the enlightened many. We have said that the encouragement of community should, along with meeting need, be the central purpose of housing policy. It follows that it should therefore be the obligation of all social landlords. A statutory provision for the Mutual Aid Compact would mean that all social landlords would go down the neighbourly route. So the obligation to offer the Mutual Aid Compact would be with social landlords, but, as we have said, the statutory provisions would not extend to a refusal of housing or evicting of those who do not sign or fulfil the Mutual Aid Compact. It would extend solely to requiring all social landlords to offer the Mutual Aid Compact to new tenants; existing tenants would be offered the Compact on a voluntary basis. In this way the law could encourage a new custom without infringing the rights of those who need housing at least to get an offer of a home as they do currently. The law would not be being used to coerce tenants into mutual aid, but to ensure a national approach by social landlords. The analogy with the home-school contract is very clear.

This combination of a law that applied to all social landlords and a Compact that would enshrine an expectation of the tenants, but not a draconian, enforceable requirement, would in our view strike the proper balance between ensuring that an objective of national housing policy is consistently implemented and achieved while recognising the essentially voluntary and generous nature of mutual aid. We said in Chapter 1 we would challenge the view that the formal can never support the informal; that they are wholly separate and distinct. We have challenged it and suggested ways in which the formal (transferrable mutuality points and a statutory requirement on social landlords to introduce a Mutual Aid Compact) could encourage the informal (family, neighbourhood and community) not as a substitute for but as a substantial addition to the many enabling interventions that are already being made by social land-lords, some of which we have described.

MUTUAL AID HOUSING ADVISORY CENTRE

We have set out in general terms here our thoughts on how communities could be built upon and mutual aid encouraged. But it would not be the same everywhere. Local approaches and local solutions will be needed. Social landlords will need to look for activities that meet the needs and aspirations of local people in their area. In order to facilitate the development of local approaches we would like to see a Mutual Aid Housing Advisory Centre. The work of the centre would be to join in partnership with social land-lords in building mutual aid where it has been diminished by social change, poverty or unemployment (though mutual aid very often thrives in areas of poverty and unemployment, because it does not come with a price tag that cannot be afforded and may be almost the only resource still available). Apart from retrieving and rebuild-ing mutual aid, the centre would also work with newly established communities in social housing to build on the ties and bonds of mutuality that exist amongst families, friends and neighbours. The Centre would help social landlords to make sure that the policies, procedures and other interventions by the landlord – the way the housing is let, the area is managed, the community developed, the landscaping and the environment established and maintained – sus-tained neighbourliness and mutuality and did not inadvertently undermine or destroy it. The Centre would be like no other advisory agency on community development. Mutual aid would be in its name and in its specific nature.

Some may suggest that the Centre might have one other func-tion: to establish a new form of social housing provider – mutual aid housing associations. We should stress again and again our prefer-ence that the mutual aid arrangements we propose be taken on by existing providers of social housing.

MUTUAL AID HOUSING ASSOCIATIONS?

As we have explained, our proposals that social needs ought to form part of the system by which social housing is prioritised, and the introduction of a Mutual Aid Compact, could be achieved by existing social landlords. That would be very much to be preferred. We want existing tenants drawn into mutual aid relationships where possible, not just new tenants in distant and ideal communities not yet built. We also want to see an integration of approaches to the building and management of social housing with other social objectives – combating social exclusion and building strong, cohesive communities.

Three strands of social policy need to be brought together for mutual aid to increase significantly. Firstly, new social housing is needed and that has been much discussed in this book. The way in which it is managed, rents are set and services are provided are all areas in need of review to reflect the changing contemporary and social context. In Chapter 2 we gave examples, both big and small, of some of the "re-inventions" of social housing that are already taking place or being considered. The worst estates need local management and sensitive allocations. Rents must be affordable and not consign the poor to a poverty trap. Services must reflect the higher standards of quality and value for money that all consumers now expect. Much work has been done by policy makers, academics and social landlords in all these areas to plan for change. The overarching purpose of these changes and improvements in housing policy is the building of sustainable communities.

Secondly, creating jobs, increasing income and, more specifically, improving the prospects of the young and the long-term unemployed for leaving welfare and going into work is a fundamental area of social policy which cannot be neglected any longer. If it were to be, social disorder with seismic consequences might, in the view of the great economist and writer, JK Galbraith, be the consequence.

> Tranquillity has depended on the comparison with previous discomfort. With time that comparison fades, and also with time the past promise of escape from relative privation, of upward movement, diminishes. This especially could be the consequence of a slowing or shrinking economy and even more of prolonged recession or depression...No one should be surprised if this

should, someday, breed a violent reaction. It has always been one of the tenets of high comfort that the uncomfortable accept peacefully, even gladly, their fate.[13]

Bringing together housing and employment generation could encourage the stability of residence that is one of the building blocks of community we described in Chapter 3. Where macro-economic shifts mean that employment is lost locally on a mass scale by the closure of a factory or an office more will be needed than job creation in local services, but a contribution can be made and that will be invaluable to those, however small a number, who get a job opportunity locally, rather than facing a gloomy and extended period of unemployment. Mutual aid can also be a means to widening the networks of unemployed people, thereby, as Perri 6 has observed, improving their economic chances.

Local exchange trading schemes are needed so that people could get some of the things through mutual aid that they could not always afford to pay for in money. Credit unions will allow the money they have to be saved efficiently and, where more money was needed, it could be borrowed in a cost effective way. Along with local job generation, there are elements here of local anti-poverty strategies which would not only take people from welfare to work, but would also not add to the costs of welfare and the potential for breeding dependency on it.

The third area of social policy with which we are concerned is social care. We can be certain that there are very large potential savings for the welfare state. The cost of residential care for old people, and for disabled people of younger ages, is very large. In 1996 the average residential care charge was £230 per week for a shared room and £247 for a private room. The average weekly nursing care charge was £323 for a shared room, £347 for a private room.[14] Social isolation is frequently one of the main reasons why people go into expensive homes at all even though they may very much wish not to. However much professional domiciliary care they are given by social workers, home helps, chiropodists, community nurses, physiotherapists and others, if old people still feel on their own as they often do and – in fact are on their own for much of the time with no family for support – they are that much more liable to enter a Home and raise the cost of looking after them by something of a quantum leap. The extended family, where it is in evidence, and other carers keep people at home and out of Homes. The extended family also reduces the cost of new care packages devised by care managers from social service departments. Moreover, the cost of care packages can be reduced if a supportive family which has been far away moves closer.

Even in the most extreme circumstances of terminal illness it would seem that people still prefer the care of the community, not just care in the community. Peter Tebbit, senior adviser with the National Council for Hospice and Specialist Palliative Care Services, feels after several years of running a hospice in western England serving a population of around 250,000 that patients from rural areas seemed more willing to travel comparatively long distances to the hospice for day care than their city counterparts. Village communities, he had found, were also often more supportive to patients – and their families – who were being cared for in their own homes.[15]

There would also be potential savings if more of the 1.4 million single parents with 2.3 million children between them were able to go out to do paid work. The child care they need might come from members of the extended family or other friends and carers if they live near enough or if they need to move nearer by using the proposed mutuality points. It would be the same if they had the benefit of a child minder or a crèche. Social security payments would be saved and tax revenues increased.

Nobody knows exactly how great the savings could be for the welfare state. Nor can it be known whether the savings would in due course be enough to reduce the total costs which will otherwise rise ineluctably with the sheer rise in numbers of old people, particularly those over 85. But demographic change is complex. It has produced, and is producing, more of the elderly elderly but also the young elderly, who are the chief source of extra informal carers for dependent people at each end of the age spectrum, the young young and the elderly elderly. We know that there are going to be more people who have retired from paid work who will have the capacity to do unpaid work as family volunteers, or other volunteers. What nobody knows, without further research and piloting, is how many of the extra people will be willing to undertake the task.

We would want existing social landlords to build new settlements in a way that would allow three generations to live nearby one another. They would also seek to encourage stability of residence and proximity. Social needs would feature alongside housing need in the allocations and mutual aid would be a key aspect alongside the tenancy agreement. As far as possible, local housing and environmental services would be organised and delivered on a mutual aid basis or through community businesses by the residents themselves. This would lead to lower rents, with the beneficial impact that that will have on making the poverty trap more shallow and encouraging stability of residence.

In addition we hope that people's care needs could be met at least in part by neighbours and local people. This might be done on a voluntary or mutual aid basis, organised in the way we have already described, or it may need more professional input. Even in those circumstances we would still like to see local people providing some of such professional services, receiving training where necessary. So there would also be job creation opportunities in caring for old and disabled people, as well as children. Not only would the community grow but also the local economy would grow.

It is important to stress that we have seen all the elements above in one place or another which we have visited during the writing of this book. What we have not seen is them all present in one place. The integration of strands of social policy currently standing alone sometimes oblivious to consequences elsewhere in the social economy, may be part of a case for a new kind of organisation, though, as has been said, it would be very much to be preferred if existing organisations would embody and integrate these ideas into their relationsips with their current tenants and, more crucially, the relationships that tenants have with one another.

All of these measures taken together by existing or new providers would build that most crucial asset still neglected and elusive in social housing – social capital – which is the fount, in the end, not just of neighbourliness and community, whose generation we wish to see as the overarching purpose of housing policy but, in the minds of many, of much economic activity.

> One of the most important lessons we can learn from an examination of economic life is that a nation's well-being, as well as its ability to compete, is conditioned by a single, pervasive cultural characteristic: the level of trust inherent in a society.[16]

According to the historian and sociologist Francis Fukuyama, whose views are quoted above, "Those who pay attention to community may indeed become the most efficient of all."

We have taken a step along this road in Bradford, West

Yorkshire. We have, together with Manningham Housing Association and the Anchor Trust, proposed a new mutual aid housing scheme. One hundred families will, we hope, form the nucleus of a utopian community beyond the Millennium. A small recognition of this work has been given by the Institute for Social Inventions which has judged the project the best social innovation in the housing category of their international awards in 1997. But it is not just one site, however dramatic a demonstration it would be, that is needed. We want to see the principles and practice of mutual aid incorporated in all local authority and housing association schemes, old and new.

*   *   *

In this chapter we have discussed some of the means by which informal mutual aid could be encouraged. We have called it informal; at the point where it happens, if it happens at all, the sort of aid we have been thinking of is certainly informal. But just as the informal can sometimes encourage the formal so it can happen the other way round. The formal can encourage the informal, as we have been illustrating by the two changes in formal policy that we have been recommending. We have proposed that, wherever possible, there should be a marriage between social and housing needs. This will preserve and enhance the family and other ties and bonds which put the guts into mutual aid. And for those who are not joined together in these ways, they could be joined by means of a Mutual Aid Compact alongside tenancy agreements.

CHAPTER five

The Wider Community

A s it has turned out, the policy proposals we have made so far, in Chapter 4 especially, have been directed more to local authorities than to housing associations. The proposal for mutuality points awarded to people for their social needs being transferable from them to the other people who could satisfy their needs is directed at local authorities as well as at the government. The new Mutual Aid Compact which people are to be encouraged to sign is for both types of social housing landlord, housing association and local authority. We believe that they can be the pioneers for the country generally in establishing and encouraging more of the mutual aid that already exists. In this chapter we are moving outwards from social housing to housing in general, from council and housing association estates to all the sorts of places which make up the United Kingdom, including owner-occupied housing.

We have already said that we are not at any point proposing anything that is completely new. Extended families are already helping their old and their young members on a vast scale, as are friends and neighbours, voluntary bodies and churches. We are merely proposing that it should be made easier for them to muster the mutual support which is the essence of family and friendship. Mutual aid is being practised everywhere outside the extended family, and could be added to. It applies to every sort of housing. You cannot go anywhere in Britain or elsewhere without finding at least some manifestation of mutual aid and, of course, its opposite. To make our point, we will give a few examples of day-to-day co-operation which tie people together and builds communities where people do not all have the same social landlord; where, indeed, they may have no landlord at all, or where the landlord may barely be relevant at all.

Everyday co-operation

We have already described in Chapter 3 how children can bring people together into communities. Other ways of bringing people together also exist. In other countries whole communities have been established in line with the ancient meeting -and-eating tradition of all cultures. In Denmark, people frustrated by the available housing options have developed a new kind of housing that "redefines the concept of neighbourhood to fit contemporary lifestyles". Tired of the isolation and impracticalities of single-family houses and flats, they have built housing that combines the autonomy of private homes with the advantages of community living. Each family or individual has a private home, but they also share common facilities with the larger group, not just a tenants' or community hall for meetings and social activities. A kitchen and a dining hall are often included, children's playrooms, workshops, guest rooms, and laundry facilities. So the level of contact between neighbours is more frequent, more varied and closer than would be the case if everything was done in private. The distinction between private and public space is being blurred by the creation of a shared private space for practical as well as leisure uses.

At that tired, fractious time of day when the children return from school and the parents have been at work or busy all day, tempers can fray. Getting a decent meal on the table is all that everybody wants, but the time between arriving home and eating can be one of the most tense and difficult moments in the family day. Co-housing, with its emphasis on eating and preparing an evening meal together on a rota basis, can help people to meet this most fundamental emotional and practical need – odd as that seems in the British context.

By 1993 more than 140 of these communities had been built in Denmark, with many more planned. They range in size from 6 to 40 households, with the majority between 15 and 33 homes. As more and more have been built, putative residents have recognised in some new settlements that the amount of shared space means that less individual private space is needed, and the homes being built have got smaller, making them cheaper to build, and therefore accessible to people on lower incomes.[1] Families wanting less rather than more private spaces fundamentally reverses the general trend of the last hundred years. There are very few examples of that! Much of Denmark's co-housing is not social housing. People have saved, borrowed, built and paid back. Residents in co-housing communities very often have other shared concerns – a concern for environmentally-friendly living, or wanting to live in a place where cars do not dominate. So perhaps it is not just social housing estates where there is the feeling that we have been expressing: that things done together will add up to more than things done alone and apart.

For some people, knowing your neighbours and meeting together, even to eat regularly, is not enough. Misfortune can also create a tie of greater depth than superficial good neighbourliness and it is liable to dog everyone at sometime – an illness, an errant or rebellious young person, a divorce or a death. Funerals particularly strengthen the ties between those that remain as a small compensation for the loss of the one that has gone.[2] At such times mutual aid comes into its own, above all in families, but between long-standing friends too. Misfortune can also bring people together in permanent organisation like the many hundreds of self-help bodies in health that have sprung up in this century, some of them with hundreds of thousands of members. The College of Health has lists of at least 2,300 of them, ranging from the Parkinson's Disease Society to the National Schizophrenia Fellowship and the National Autistic Society.

In more ordinary times an interest may become a shared interest – wine-making, pigeon fancying, embroidery, organising and attending car boot fairs or any one of a variety of sports from football to bowls, as player or spectator. Smaller groups can gather to pursue these interests and link up with people further afield with the same interest, and on the Internet with like-minded people the world over.

It is an ill wind... and collective complaints can have their positive side. "How do we stop irresponsible drivers using our road as a speedy rat run to avoid the main road? Could we persuade the council to install speed bumps, or perhaps that would make it worse? What is to be done about the terrible state of the park? And as for the dog mess, it has reached intolerable proportions. Can nothing be done about piles of black bags in the street?" These are not imagined examples. Salford University's 1993 research[3] reports that traffic management and parking disputes, rubbish collection and dog mess are prime causes of frustration and dissatisfaction. We saw them all at work at first hand in North Kensington (as described in Chapter 2) affecting, equally, social housing tenants, tenants of private landlords, and owner-occupiers. Tens of thousands of pounds were needed for the transformation of one street, known as the Canyon because it looks like a desolate, steep-sided causeway. On one side the houses have over the years reversed their aspect as the residents decided to look out on what were previously their rear garden. On the other side there are no porches, just huge, flat-fronted "cliffs". The traffic streams down a wide street, "a rat run". Residents were fed up with rubbish dumped everyday on the street because there was nowhere to store it in the home and only twice weekly collections by the council. Broken bags attract real rats which race the cars down the street. Funds have been raised by the community groups to build new bin stores and build porches on the front of houses. The road is to be narrowed and the traffic calmed.

There are usually specific local issues as well. In North Kensington prostitutes had left the phone numbers of the telephone boxes in All Saints Piazza on cards inside boxes around Bayswater and Paddington. So punters rang these boxes and the prostitutes awaited their calls. Sometimes the prostitutes were not there, but the punters still called. Drug dealing too had reached epidemic and frightening proportions. Through the local residents' forum people had come together to tackle these problems – redesigning and rebuilding the piazza to make it safer and to encourage more people to use it and campaigning for the telephone boxes to be removed. The future is a little brighter, but not for prostitutes and drug dealers.

In Chapter 2 we gave some examples of tenants' halls and community centres being places where people can come together and mutual aid might be the result. In Chapter 3 we described how nurseries and primary schools can be the focus for people to meet and get to know one another, perhaps forming lasting relationships. In this chapter we have talked about places to meet and eat. There are other buildings which are a focus for community life. There are 8,500 village halls in Britain in which 400 kinds of activities are regularly conducted. The Millennium Commission has awarded ACRE (Action with Communities in Rural England) £10 million towards the cost of renovating or rebuilding up to 400 village halls by the year 2000. The equivalent of £35 million worth of volunteer time and effort goes into these buildings and these activities.[4] As for the churches and other places of worship, those have traditionally stood at the geographical heart of the community and been designed in an architectural style to emphasise both the centrality to the neighbourhood and higher spiritual aspirations. These architectural and social themes exist in all the great religions of the world, not just Christianity and certainly not just in Britain.

Despite their highly visible presence, it has become common to bewail falling church attendances. What goes relatively unremarked is the wider social role that churches have always played and continue to play. Health, education and housing have all benefitted from the energies and creativity of many social entrepreneurs who in the first instance took their inspiration from religion. We have already commented that churches can be a source of contacts for job seekers. But they are also a more informal social centre. In Thomas Hardy's *Under the Greenwood Tree*, written more than a hundred years ago, choir practice was the focus for a regular social encounter, which often culminated in a good deal of slightly inebriated merriment, and the social tradition continues, though not always involving drinking.

Small, deliberately undramatic illustrations can make our point about how communities can be brought together and wide coverage of local people can be achieved in the very general interests of neighbourliness and mutual aid. St Faith's Church in North Dulwich, an ordinary London suburban parish church, attracts 100 people to its services every Sunday, but more than 1,000 people a week use the community centre that has been built from the old church hall, most of them not church-goers and many of them from non-Christian communities. In a community of less than 9,000 people (the figure that the Anglican church uses to broadly define a parish) this is a significant proportion of local people and if one took into account the other local people known to the users of the centre, the network surrounding the centre would cover well over half of the residents in the neighbourhood. The contacts generated are not just social. Mutual aid forms part of the organisation of the activities of the centre, as well as the relationships that are nurtured from the Church, the visiting of the sick being a very obvious example. So much so in fact that in some places this dual religious and social responsibility has been formalised. At Charterhouse in Southwark, an Anglican church and community project in Bermondsey, the work of the priest in charge is formally divided half and half between religious duties and organising local volunteers and befrienders. Black churches too have grown up in many areas with significant ethnic minority communities. They are not just a focus for prayer and worship, but also for the organisation of multilateral mutual aid as we described in Chapter 1.

Two key features of churches and religious centres make them well suited to be centres for mutual aid. Firstly they exist everywhere in the country. Churches are amongst the very few organisations which have a local member of staff *resident* in many communities in the country, small or large, rural or urban. Secondly, the church, as in the case of St Faith's, sits at the centre of a social network that can, at its best, achieve almost universal coverage across a whole neighbourhood. These are remarkable, unsung achievements, even for those without religious belief. It is with this in mind that we suggest in the discussion below on community plans that churches and religious centres may in some areas be the hub of the arrangements we propose for community audits of social needs and the capacity for meeting them.

One view of modern society is that it is full of atomised, anonymous, asocial, amoral individuals, isolated from each other in a lonely crowd. But though that is how it seems in some places, it is by no means uniformly like that, and we have just been giving a few examples of the vitality which is still evident in mutual aid of different kinds. The question now is about some of the ways in which mutuality could be further encouraged not just in new settlements but in the country generally. The question, even more precisely, is what could be the counterpart of the Mutual Aid Compact for people in any kind of housing. The obligation can arise freely, based on trust and goodwill, without being worthless as we have shown in these examples.

COMMUNITY PLANS

Mutual aid will best be considered as a response on the part of citizens to a new proposal made in Labour's general election manifesto for local authority action. The community plan is the "promise" of the local authority to its residents. If councils are going to state what they are doing for the community and how far they have fallen short, reached or exceeded their targets, in return people should say what they are going to do in the form of mutual aid and commitment to the community. We envisage that the commitment would be implemented through and by the churches, existing volunteer centres, community development trusts and other voluntary bodies. It would not be right for the citizen response to be organised by local authorities for then the local authorities would be at both sides of the table at once, explaining to citizens what the authority intended to do and helping the citizens to put together what would be their side of a community component. It would be more convincing if there was a measure of independence for the organisation on the side of the citizen. This is where the churches and voluntary bodies could come onto the scene to give expression to whatever it was that people were prepared to do for the sake of the community.

It could help if the voluntary bodies that were ready to co-operate had a common form of mutual aid commitment for their locality. The Mutual Aid Compact set out in the previous chapter could be the basis for it, but with every one of the participating bodies being able to adapt the contents for its purposes. In some districts where voluntary bodies are well organised and one of them was prepared to be the lead body, it would be the focus for the community organisation in general. The whole effort of community regeneration would become more focused if the lead body, in collaboration with others, would make an annual community audit of social needs and the capacity for meeting them, both from professional services and from volunteers. The community audit would identify people's unmet needs and the willingness of volunteers to join in meeting them. The audit could be used for collating opinions about the local community plan as well as identifying social needs and volunteers. Some lead bodies (or others to whom the task was delegated) might choose to approach every household in their area. Others might combine a sample survey for interview with self-administered questionnaires delivered to homes. Others might rely on the questionnaire alone, thinking that on the whole it would be the activists, or the people ready to be activists, who would be the first to respond.

The community audit would need to be financed, and so would such special staff as would be required to supervise and follow up on the audit. No doubt there would often be local funds that could be raised – although much more readily in well-off districts than in impoverished ones. But it would help a great deal if there could be some support from the government, or from the National Lottery.

NEIGHBOURHOOD WATCH AS A MODEL

For local action, Neighbourhood Watch schemes are a model for what could be done in many places. There are at the latest count 150,000 of them in the country as a whole, all in response to a need which is as local as it is near-universal – crime prevention. The idea behind them all is to generate self-help on the part of local people and increase the willingness of volunteers to look after each other in such a way that crime is reduced.

The local police force typically has a Neighbourhood Watch co-ordinator on its staff. His or her job is to support existing schemes and help to start new ones. A new one is brought into existence when a local street or village co-ordinator is ready to give some time to the scheme and to link with the police. When the possibilities look hopeful a paid support officer, not in uniform, attends a street meeting and maybe shows a video produced by the local police headquarters on how schemes can work best. The video has plenty of tips in it about how people can identify and deal with bogus callers either in person or on the telephone and become more aware of suspicious strangers. Home Office leaflets on Neighbourhood Watch may be handed out and stickers that people can put on their windows. After the meeting everything depends on the local co-ordinator. He or she has a fast Crime Link over the phone with the local police station.

Could some of these local co-ordinators spread themselves to include mutual aid? They can already come very close to it since they, and the other local residents involved in the scheme, have to be on the lookout for vulnerable local people, for example, elderly people in ground floor flats which are not overlooked by anyone else. It would be only a step from there to considering how these vulnerable people could be supported in more ways than locking windows and strengthening front doors.

Some of the Home Office publications have made the same kind of point about ways in which Neighbourhood Watch could bring the community closer together:

- Visit elderly or sick residents – you could also make links with local doctors and organisations like Help the Aged or the British Red Cross.
- Liaise with the youth service to develop facilities for young people such as youth clubs or holiday play schemes.[5]
- As many as 20,000 Neighbourhood Watch schemes around

the country include Street Watch elements. This term covers many different activities ranging from transport and escort services for elderly people, walking a specific route regularly, keeping an eye out for suspicious traffic and reporting it all to the police.[6]

The criticism that has been made of Neighbourhood Watch Schemes is that they are more common in relatively well-off areas than in the less well-off. All the same there are many lessons to be learned from them.

REDISTRIBUTION TO THE LESS WELL-OFF

Britain is a country as well as a little universe of localities. The whole has to come to the aid of the part. Everyone knows that some districts, in and out of the inner cities, are so miserable that all hope has almost fled. We had evidence enough of this from our own survey and from some of the follow-up interviews which were done. An estate we visited in a small town in the North West of England is a case in point. Couples described how they could never go out together because a house left empty, even briefly, was more likely to be broken into. If you reported a crime you were more likely to have a break in. You did not look people in the face when you left your house because you did not know who were your friends and who were your enemies. There were signs everywhere proclaiming "No Ball Games", but what were the youngsters expected to play with if not a ball of some kind? The sad day had come when the decision had been taken to build a substantial wall around the entire estate to exclude the miscreants! The estate, like a medieval town, has become a fortress.

Or take another example, admittedly extreme – the Ocean Estate in Tower Hamlets.[7] A survey team there explored the connection between housing and health. Most of the flats were oozing damp with nowhere to dry clothes, "The family lives in appalling conditions. Every room was streaming with water and dampness. She is in constant pain and visits her doctor constantly. The Council have said they will repair the damp within seven to eight months." The damp in other flats made the cold worse. "The flat is always cold. The heating system is inadequate in the face of the damp. Additionally they cannot afford to heat the flat properly." Many of the blocks also suffer from infestation. "The infestation comes and goes. At the first visit there were cockroaches which were treated successfully by the second visit. By the third visit the flat was full of Pharaoh's Ants." "Infestation is getting worse, it's disgusting. Cockroaches get in the food and they have to throw it away and cook again." No amount of Mutual Aid Compacts and earnest pleas for the regeneration of community will touch the most miserable places in the country. If they are to revive, they need a kick-start through new resources being brought to their aid. Once people there see that some positive improvements are being made to their housing there is a chance of morale beginning to rise.

We cite these two examples (which could be multiplied by thousands) to show that however much mutual aid there is on a local scale, to make it effective there has to be mutual aid on a national scale. Not everything can be achieved by means of self-help or local mutual aid. Public services which are not just a safety net for the poor, but are based on the principle of universal entitlement – like the National Health Service and schooling – are a recognition of this. The rich pay more; the poor may pay nothing, but the entitlement is the same. In the lower reaches of society people will only be able to help each other effectively if they in their turn are helped from outside a community where self-help needs to be underpinned by help for those who have less from those who have more.

AFTERWORD

Recommendations

- Building communities should, along with meeting housing need, be a central policy purpose of social housing.

- Social housing should be allocated according to social as well as housing needs. Mutuality points could be transferred from people needing support to those willing to give it.

- All social landlords should be required to incorporate social needs in allocations and encourage mutual aid between tenants and neighbours by offering the Mutual Aid Compact to all new tenants.

- Some of the available capital receipts should be given over to the employment of community development co-ordinators by housing associations, local authorities and voluntary bodies to promote and develop mutual aid in their neighbourhoods.

- Social landlords should encourage mutual aid. This would mean providing more new social housing for three generations with a mutualist approach to housing and estate management. It would mean encouraging local job creation and organising social care locally for children and elderly and disabled people, provided by volunteers as well as paid professionals. A Mutual Aid Housing Advisory Centre could assist and enable social landlords to develop informal and formal mutual aid by giving them advice and encouragement.

- In areas of mixed tenure housing, churches and other local voluntary bodies should undertake community audits to bring together those in need of support with those volunteers willing to give it. Local authorities should incorporate the findings of the community audits into the proposed community plans.

NOTES

Chapter 1

1 Hutton W, *The State We're In*, Vintage, 1995
2 Holmans A, *Housing Demand and Need in England 1991 – 2011*, Joseph Rowntree Foundation, 1995
3 *Annual Review 1996-1997*, Housing Corporation
4 Wilcox S, *Housing Review 1996 – 1997*, Joseph Rowntree Foundation, 1996
5 Survey of Users, CRASH, 1997
6 *Op cit*, Wilcox S
7 As quoted in *Housing Today*, 17 July 1997
8 Power A and Tunstall R, *Swimming Against the Tide: Polarisation and progress on 20 unpopular council estates, 1980 – 1995*, Joseph Rowntree Foundation, 1995
9 Page D, *Building for Communities*, Joseph Rowntree Foundation, 1993 and *Developing Communities*, Sutton Hastoe Housing Association, 1994
10 See Leach *et al*, *Children and Violence*, Gulbenkian Foundation, 1996
11 Power A, *Estates on the Edge: The social consequences of mass housing in Northern Europe*, Macmillan, 1997
12 Woods R A, *The Neighbourhood in Social Reconstruction*, Eighth Annual Meeting of the American Sociological Society, 1913. Quoted in Park R E and Burgess E W, *The City*, University of Chicago Press, 1967, p7
13 Lansbury G, *Looking Backwards and Forwards*, Blackie, 1935
14 *Economist*, 21-27 June 1997, p36
15 *Fraud and Lodging: Tackling fraud and error in housing benefit* and *Measures to combat housing before fraud*, Audit Commission and National Audit Office, 1997
16 Richards E, *Paying for Long-Term Care*, Institute for Public Policy Research, 1996. Quoted in Kirkwood A and Astle J, *Long-Term Care*, Institute of Community Studies, 1996
17 *General Household Survey: Carers in 1990*, The Stationery Office
18 Sykes R and Leather P, *Grey Matters*, Anchor Trust, 1997
19 Titmuss R, *The Gift Relationship*, LSE Books, 1997

Chapter 2

1 *Op cit*, Power A and Tunstall R, *Swimming Against the Tide*
2 *Ibid*
3 Power A and Tunstall R, *Dangerous Disorders: Riots and violent disturbances in 13 areas of Britain 1991-1992*, Joseph Rowntree Foundation, 1997
4 *Op cit*, Page D
5 *Op cit*, Page D, *Developing Communities*, Sutton Hastoe Housing Association, 1994
6 *A Housing Plus Approach to Achieving Sustainable Communities*, Housing Corporation, 1997
7 *Inside Housing*, 25 July 1997
8 *Housing Today*, 7 August 1997
9 Largest 200 by self-contained units owned, using the Housing Corporation's 1995 listing.
10 The total potential responses were actually less than 250 because the listing naturally dates fairly quickly due to mergers, etc.
11 Housing associations were given more options when completing the questionnaire but they have been amalgamated. There were two other categories in the survey: allocations to achieve a social and economic mix, of which 40 were reported. There were 21 other projects which respondents found it difficult to classify.
12 *Competence and Accountability: Code of Governance*, National Housing Federation, 1995
13 Steele A, *The Effectiveness of Estate Agreements*, Joseph Rowntree Foundation, 1995
14 Page D, *Developing Communities* and Zipfel T and Hare L, *Multi-landlord Estates*, Joseph Rowntree Foundation, 1995
15 For Example, Peters T and Waterman R, *In Search of Excellence: Lessons from America's best run companies*, Harper & Row, New York, 1987
16 McGregor A *et al*, *Bridging the Jobs Gap: An evaluation of the Wise Group and the intermediate labour market*, Joseph Rowntree Foundation, 1997
17 The word comes from the French – *foyeurs pour jeunes travailleurs* – which can be simply translated as 'hostels for young workers'
18 *The Guardian*, 'Society', 2 May 1997

[19] Modood et al, *Ethnic Minorities in Britain*, Policy Studies Institute, 1997

[20] *Routes into Local Authority Housing*, Department of the Environment, 1994

[21] *Op cit*, Page D, *Building for Communities*

[22] *Social Justice: Strategies for national renewal*, The Report of the Commission on Social Justice, Vintage, 1994

[23] 'Banking Act Report', Unpublished, Bank of England, April 1993

[24] *Op cit*, Commission on Social Justice

[25] See *Saving for Credit: the future of credit unions in Britain*, National Consumer Council, 1994

[26] Mehta G, *Snakes and Ladders*, Secker & Warburg, 1997

Chapter 3

[1] See *Op cit*, Leach *et al*, and *The Cities*, The Methodist Church and NCH Action for Children, 1996

[2] *Community Care: Agenda for Action: A Report to the Secretary of State for Social Services*, London, HMSO, 1986, p5

[3] See also *The Cities*, NCH Action for Children and the Methodist Church, 1997

[4] Young M and Willmott P, *Family and Kinship in East London*, Penguin, 1986 edn

[5] *Social Trends 27*, The Stationery Office, 1997

[6] Daniel W W, *Maternity Rights: The experience of women*, Policy Studies Institute, 1980

[7] Willmott P, *Friendship, Networking and Social Support*, Policy Studies Institute, 1987

[8] Meltzer H, *Daycare Services for Children*, HMSO, 1994

[9] *British Social Attitudes Survey*, Social & Community Planning Research, 1995

[10] *Ibid*

[11] *Ibid*

[12] *Ibid*

[13] *Ibid*

[14] Ghate D and Daniels A, *Talking About My Generation*, National Society for the Prevention of Cruelty to Children, 1997

[15] *Op cit*, Wilcox S, p122

[16] Peach C (ed), *Ethnicity in the 1991 Census: the ethnic minority population of Great Britain*, 1995

[17] *Ibid*

18 Lemos G and West C, *Flair in the Community*, London Housing Federation,
    1996
19 Sheldon J H, *The Social Philosophy of Old Age*, Presidential Address
    to the Third Congress of the International Association of
    Gerontology, Old Age in the Modern World, London,
    Livingstone, 1955
20 Clarke P, Milbourne P, Thomas C, *Lifestyles in Rural England*,
    Rural Development Commission 1994, quoted in Simmons M,
    Landscapes – of Poverty, Lemos & Crane, 1997
21 *Op cit*, Wilmott P and Young M
22 *Op cit*, Wilcox S
23 *Op cit*, *Social Trends 27*
24 *Hackney Housing Investigated*, Commission for Racial Equality,
    1984
25 *Homelessness and Discrimination: Report of a formal investigation into
    the London Borough of Tower Hamlets*, Commission for Racial
    Equality, 1988
26 Parker J and Dugmore K, *Colour and the Allocation of GLC Housing:
    The report of the GLC lettings survey 1974-1975, Research Report
    21, GLC*
27 *Op cit*, Clarke P *et al*
28 *Op cit* Power A, *Estates on the Edge*
29 *Managing Voids and Difficult to Let Property*, Housing Corporation:
    Source 21
30 Griffiths *et al*, *Community Lettings: Local allocations policies in
    practice*, Joseph Rowntree Foundation, 1996
31 Fordham G, Kemp R and Crowsley P, *Going the Extra Mile:
    Implementing 'Housing Plus' on five London housing association
    estates*, Joseph Rowntreee Foundation, 1997
32 *Managing Vulnerability*, London Housing Federation, 1995
33 *Op cit*, Griffiths *et al*
34 Timmins N, *Financial Times*, 7 June 1997
35 *Op cit*, Wilcox S
36 *Op cit*, Clarke P *et al*
37 *Annual Review 1996-1997*, Housing Corporation
38 From CORE statistics published by the National Housing
    Federation
39 *Op cit*, *Routes into Local Authority Housing*
40 *Op cit*, Wilcox S
41 *Op cit*, Page D, *Developing Communities*

42 *Op cit*, Power A and Tunstall R, *Swimming Against the Tide*
43 *Op cit*, CORE
44 Field F, *Paying for the Future: Building a stakeholder's welfare*, Institute of Community Studies, 1996
45 Criminal Victimisation in Eleven Industralised Countries. Key findings from the 1996 International Crime Victimisation Survey prepared for the EU conference, 14 May 1997, Noordwijk, Netherlands, quoted in *The Guardian*, 27 May 1997
46 Bright J, *Turning the Tide: Crime, community and prevention*, Demos, 1997, p22
47 *The Guardian*, 15 August 1997
48 *Op cit*, Bright J, *Turning the Tide*

Chapter 4

1 Cole *et al*, *Creating communities or welfare housing: A study of new housing association developments in Yorkshire/Humberside*, Joseph Rowntree Foundation, 1997
2 Op cit, Power A, *Estates on the Edge*
3 Lemos G, *Communities within Communities*, London Housing Federation, 1995 and *Flair in the Community*, London Housing Federation, 1996
4 See also, Hunter C and Bretherton K, *Anti-social Tenants* (Arden's Housing Library), Lemos & Crane, forthcoming 1998
5 Berlin I, *Four Essays on Liberty*, OUP, 1988
6 Ministerial statement, 7 July 1997
7 *Excellence in Schools*, Department of Further Education and Employment, 1997
8 More Sir T, *Utopia*, first published 1516, Penguin, 1965, translated from Latin, Turner P, p106
9 Russell L and Scott D, *The Impact of the Contract Culture on Volunteers*, Joseph Rowntree Foundation, 1997
10 UK Domiciliary Care Market Report, 1997
11 *Residents' Democracy: A discussion paper for policy makers*, Aldbourne Associates, 1995
12 Hunter C and Selman A, *Compulsory Competitive Tendering of Housing Management* (Arden's Housing Library), Lemos & Crane, 1996
13 Galbraith J K, *The Culture of Contentment*, Penguin, 1992
14 Figures supplied by Anchor Trust, Oxford

15 Simmons M, *Landscapes – of Poverty*, Lemos & Crane, 1997
16 Fukuyama F, *Trust: The social virtues and the creation of prosperity*, Hamish Hamilton, 1996

Chapter 5

1 McCamant, Durrant and Hertzman, *Co-housing: A contemporary approach to housing ourselves*, Ten Speed Press, 1994
2 Young M and Cullen L, *A Good Death*, Routledge, 1996
3 Belgrave S, *Nuisance and Harassment* (Arden's Housing Library) Lemos & Crane, 1995
4 *Op cit*, Simmons M
5 *A Problem Solving Approach for Crime Prevention*, Home Office, 1997
6 *Welcome to Neighbourhood Watch*, Home Office, 1997
7 Ambrose P, *I Mustn't Laugh Too Much*, Centre for Urban and Regional Research, 1996

INDEX